# The Couriers 02
# Dirtbike Manifesto

## BY BRIAN WOOD AND ROB G

AiT/PLANETLAR
SAN FRANCISCO

**ALSO CHECK OUT:**

**CHANNEL ZERO**
**BY BRIAN WOOD**

**PUBLIC DOMAIN: A CHANNEL ZERO DESIGNBOOK**
**BY BRIAN WOOD**

**CHANNEL ZERO: JENNIE ONE**
**BY BRIAN WOOD AND BECKY CLOONAN**

**DEMO**
**BY BRIAN WOOD AND BECKY CLOONAN**

**COUSCOUS EXPRESS**
**BY BRIAN WOOD AND BRETT WELDELE**

**THE COURIERS** 01
**BY BRIAN WOOD AND ROB G**

**AVAILABLE FROM AIT/PLANET LAR**

**The Couriers 02: DIRTBIKE MANIFESTO**
BY BRIAN WOOD AND ROB G

Published by: AiT/Planet Lar, 2034 47th Avenue, San Francisco, CA 94116

First edition January 2004

10 9 8 7 6 5 4 3 2 1


Lettered by Ryan Yount
Cover illustrations: Rob G. Book design by Brian Wood and Whiskey Island
ISBN: 1-932051-18-X


Printed and bound in Canada by Quebecor Printing, Inc.

# The Couriers[02]
# Dirtbike Manifesto

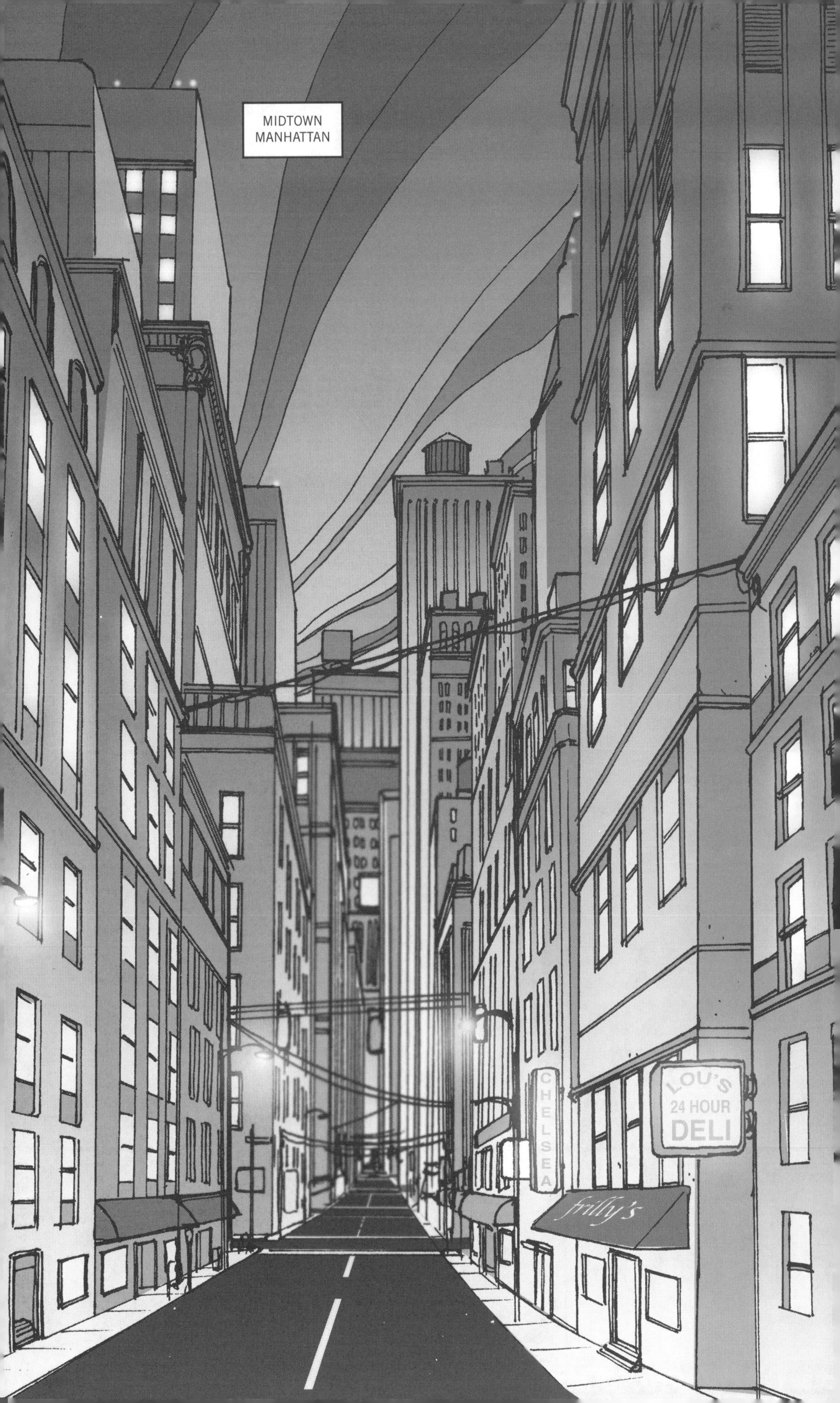
MIDTOWN
MANHATTAN
CHELSEA
LOU'S
24 HOUR
DELI
frilly's

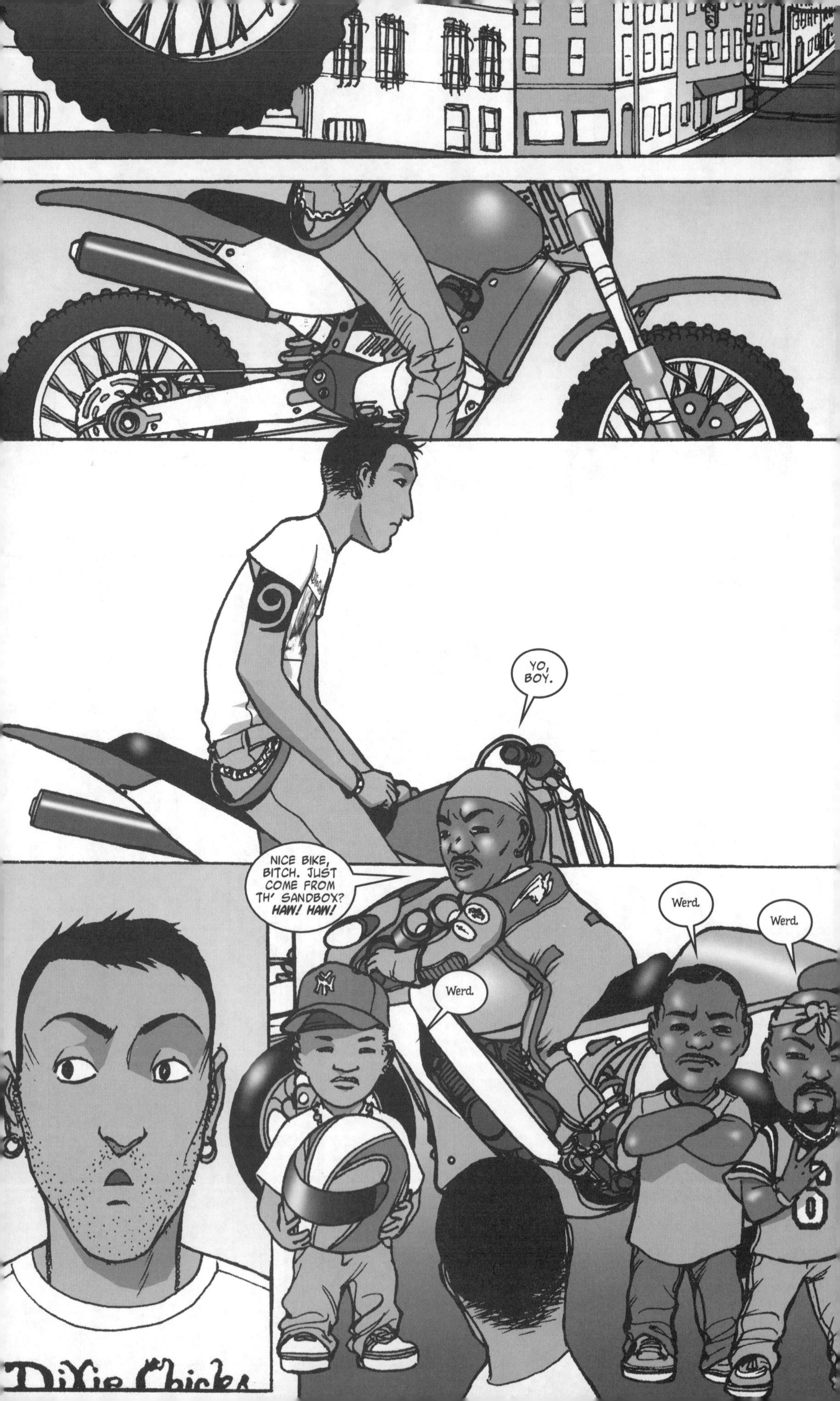

YO, BOY.
NICE BIKE, BITCH. JUST COME FROM TH' SANDBOX? ***HAW! HAW!***
Werd.
Werd.
Werd.
DiXie Chicks

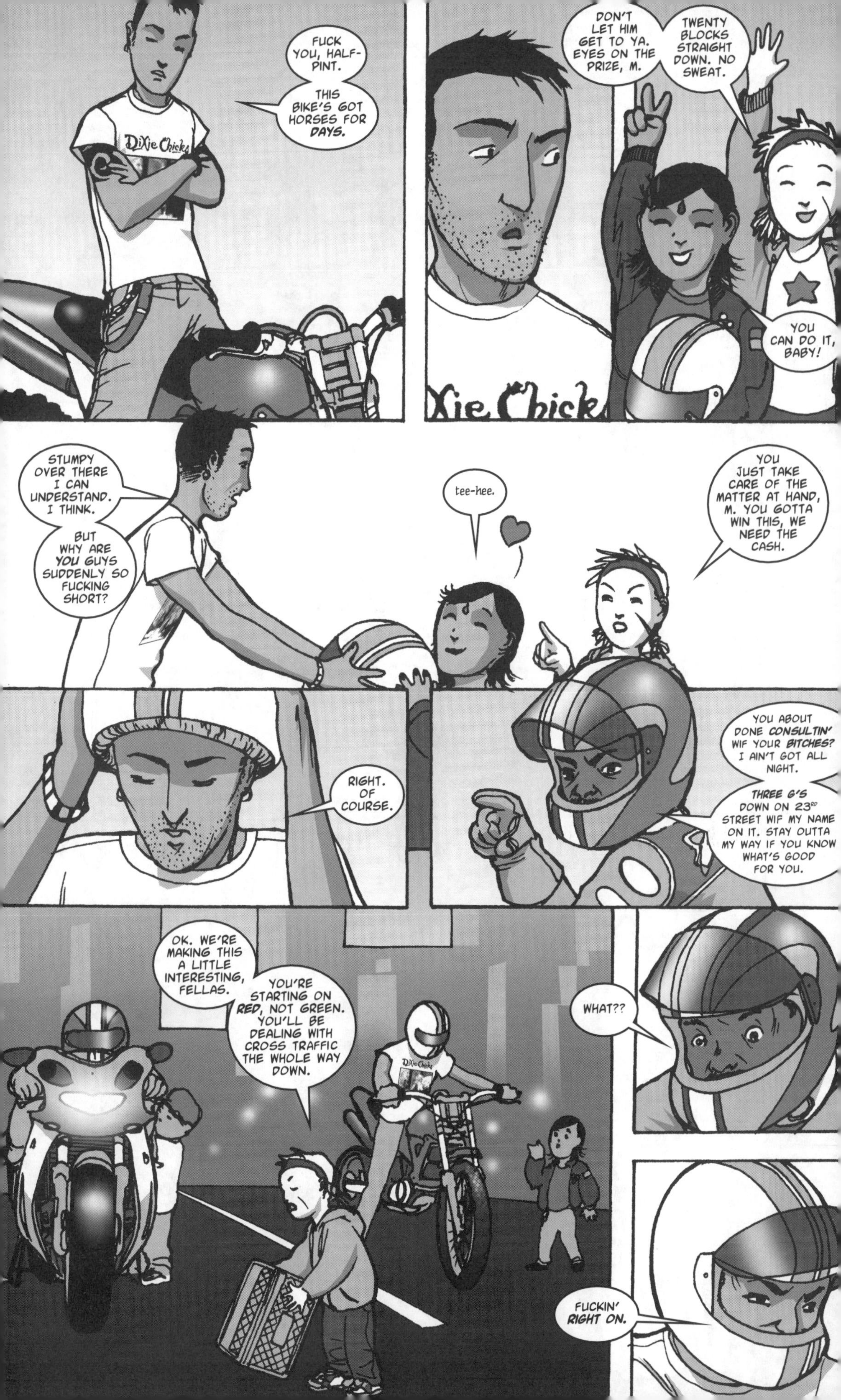
FUCK YOU, HALF-PINT.
THIS BIKE'S GOT HORSES FOR DAYS.
DiXie Chicks
DON'T LET HIM GET TO YA. EYES ON THE PRIZE, M.
TWENTY BLOCKS STRAIGHT DOWN. NO SWEAT.
YOU CAN DO IT, BABY!
STUMPY OVER THERE I CAN UNDERSTAND. I THINK.
BUT WHY ARE YOU GUYS SUDDENLY SO FUCKING SHORT?
tee-hee.
YOU JUST TAKE CARE OF THE MATTER AT HAND, M. YOU GOTTA WIN THIS, WE NEED THE CASH.
RIGHT. OF COURSE.
YOU ABOUT DONE CONSULTIN' WIF YOUR BITCHES? I AIN'T GOT ALL NIGHT.
THREE G'S DOWN ON 23RD STREET WIF MY NAME ON IT. STAY OUTTA MY WAY IF YOU KNOW WHAT'S GOOD FOR YOU.
OK. WE'RE MAKING THIS A LITTLE INTERESTING, FELLAS.
YOU'RE STARTING ON RED, NOT GREEN. YOU'LL BE DEALING WITH CROSS TRAFFIC THE WHOLE WAY DOWN.
WHAT??
FUCKIN' RIGHT ON.

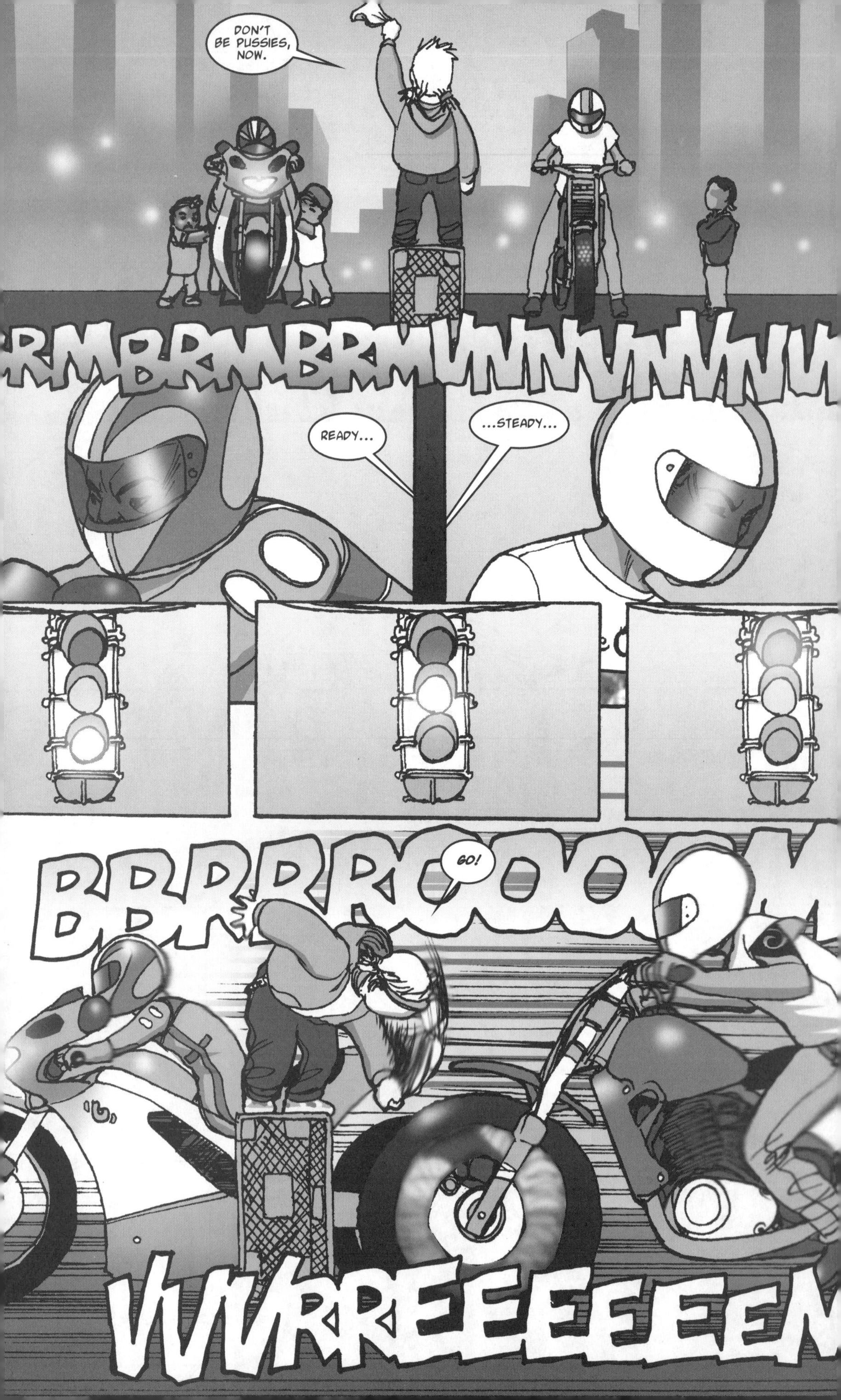
DON'T BE PUSSIES, NOW.
RMBRMBRMBRMUNNNNNNNNM
READY...
...STEADY...
GO!
BRRRROOOOOM
VVVRREEEEEEN

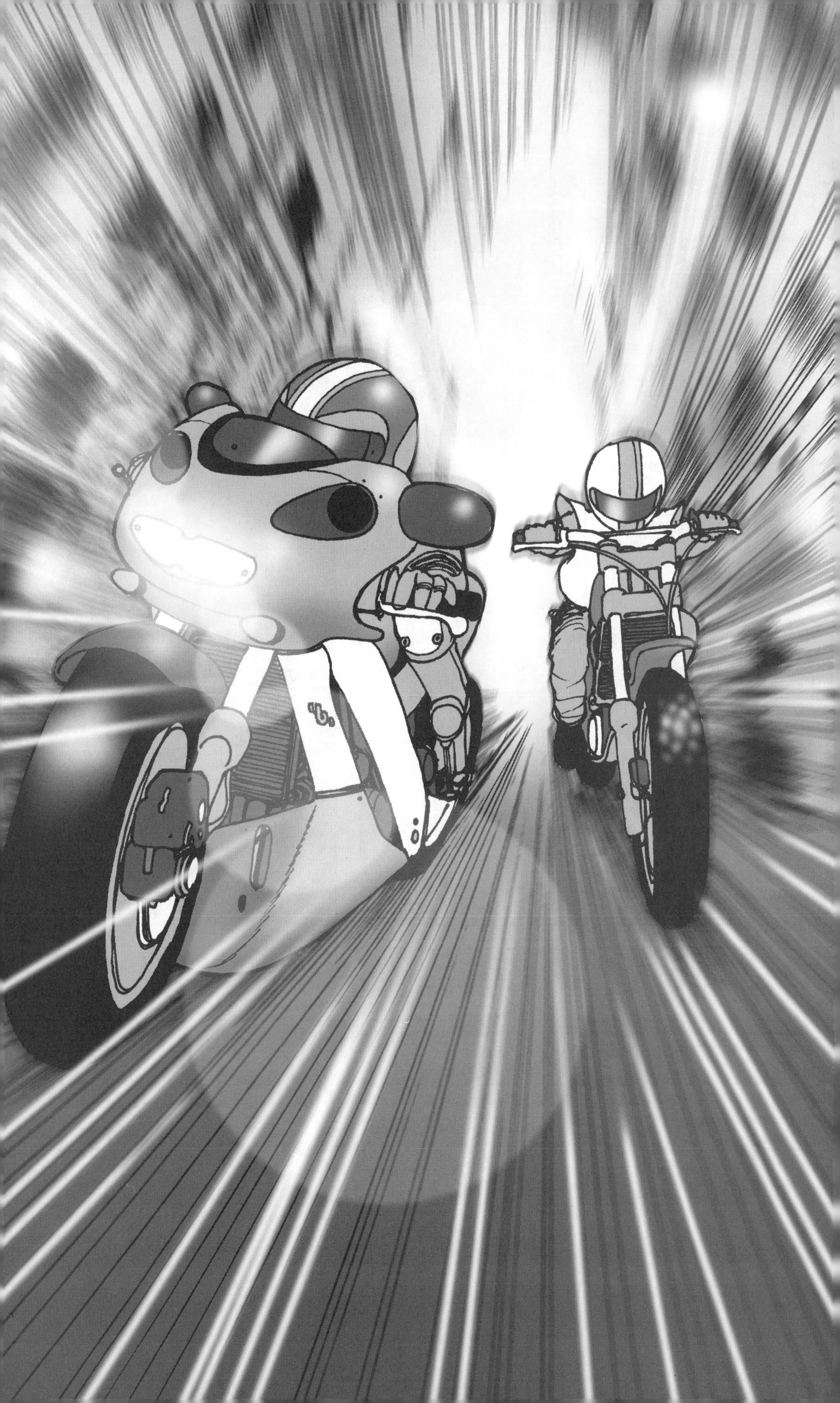

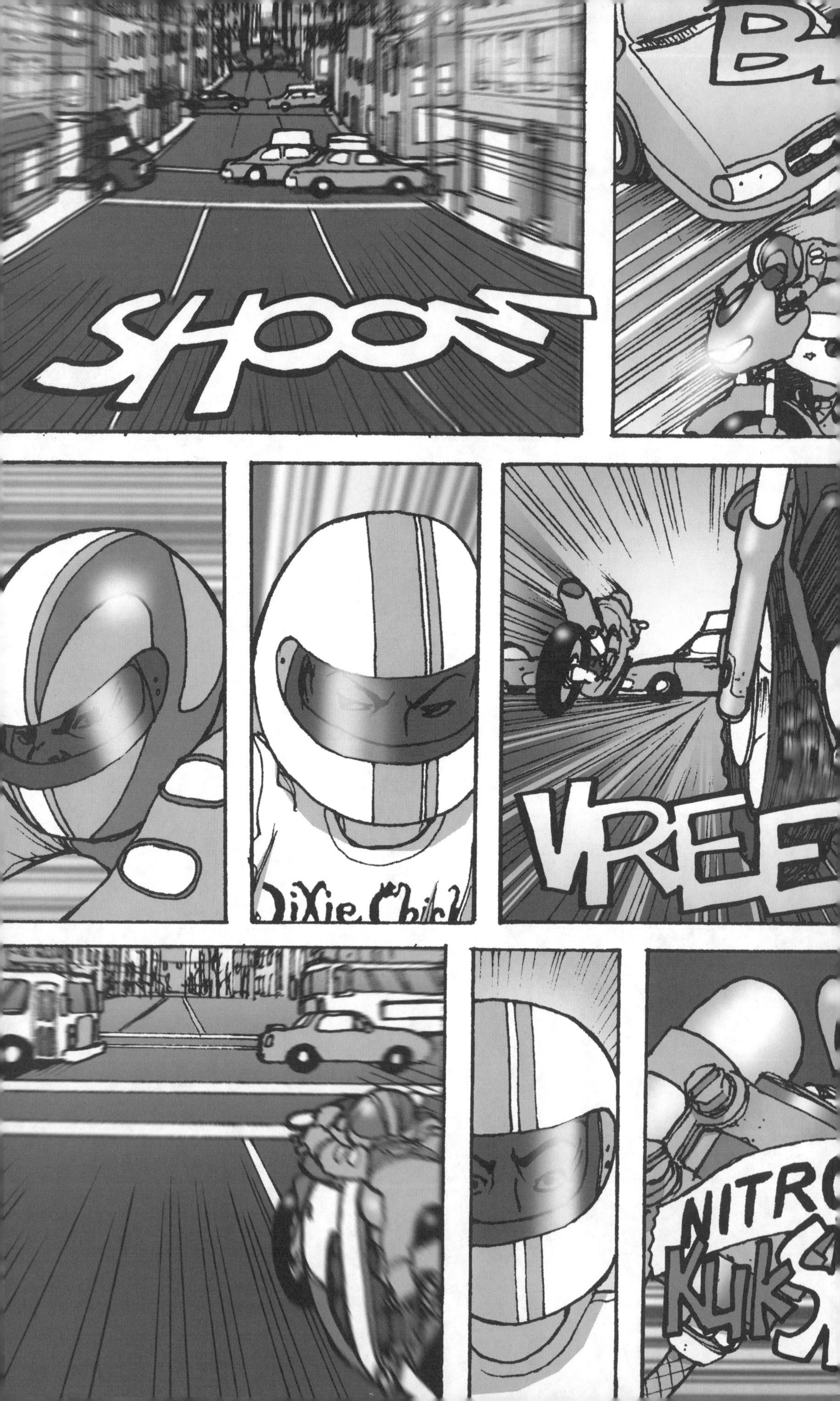
SHOOS
Dixie Chick
VREE
NITRO
KLIK

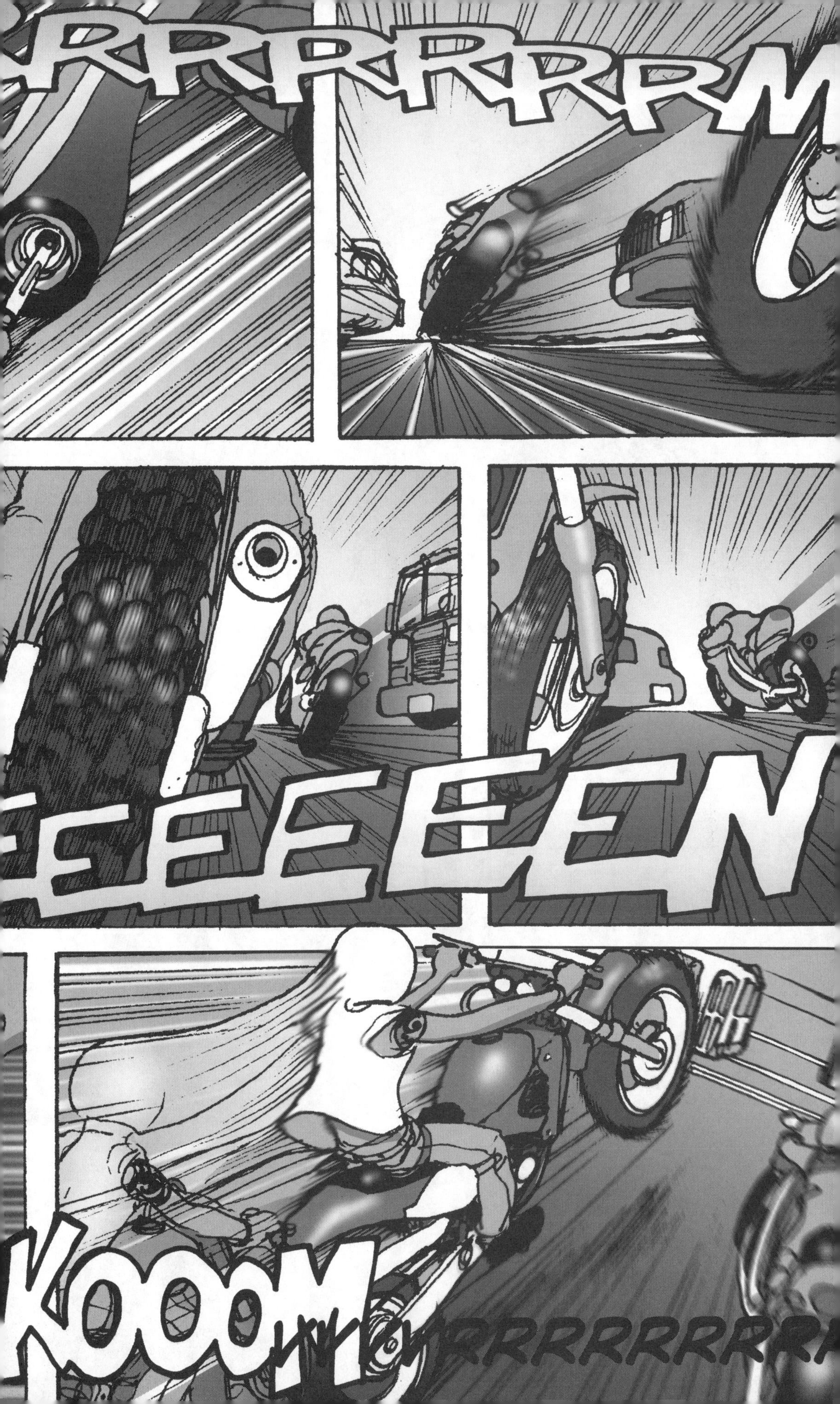
RRRRRRRM
EEEEN
KOOOM
WRRRRRRRRR

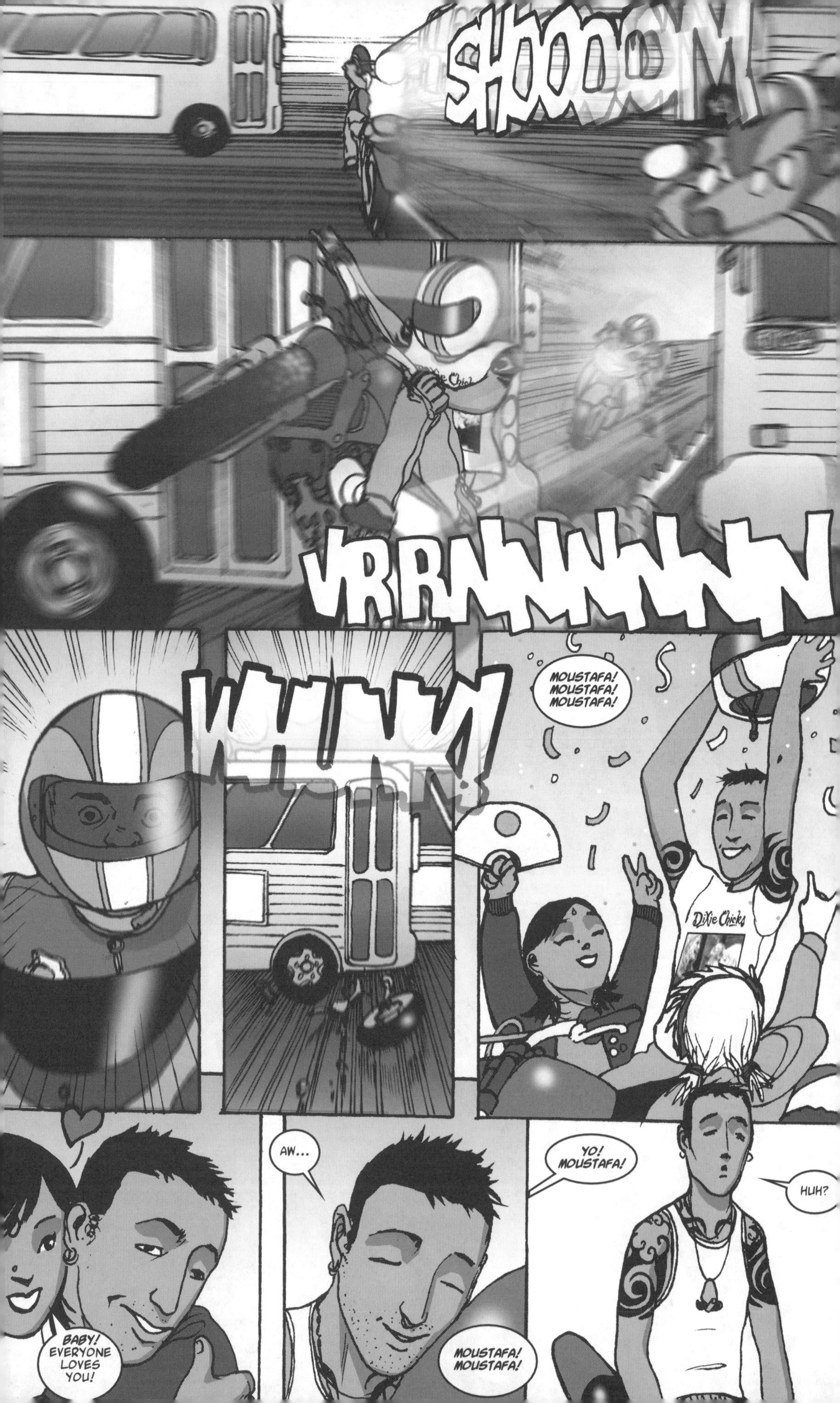
SHOOOOM!
VRRAAAAAAAAN
WHUMM!
MOUSTAFA! MOUSTAFA! MOUSTAFA!
Dixie Chicks
BABY! EVERYONE LOVES YOU!
AW...
MOUSTAFA! MOUSTAFA!
YO! MOUSTAFA!
HUH?

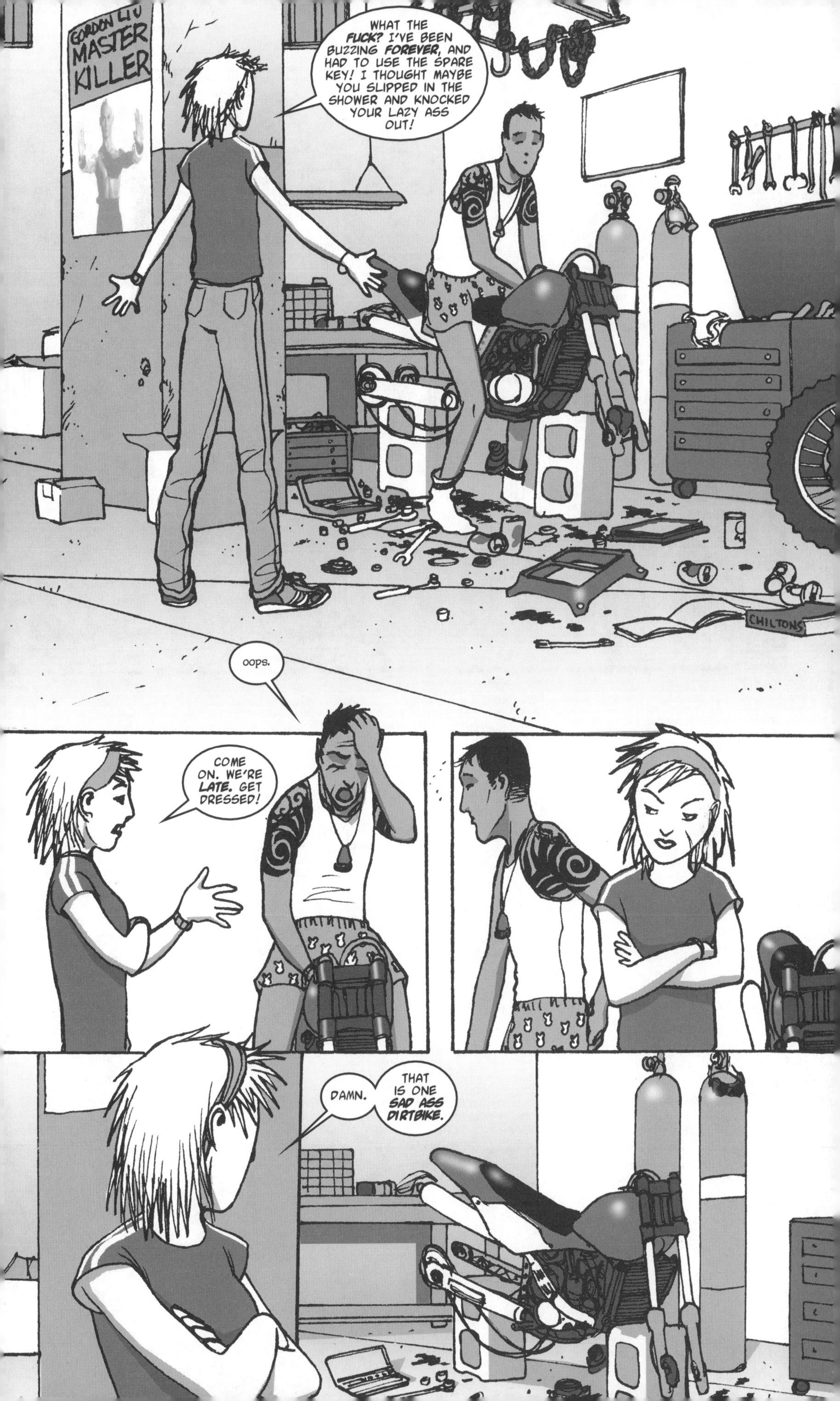
GORDON LIU
MASTER KILLER
WHAT THE FUCK? I'VE BEEN BUZZING FOREVER, AND HAD TO USE THE SPARE KEY! I THOUGHT MAYBE YOU SLIPPED IN THE SHOWER AND KNOCKED YOUR LAZY ASS OUT!
CHILTONS
oops.
COME ON. WE'RE LATE. GET DRESSED!
DAMN.
THAT IS ONE SAD ASS DIRTBIKE.

# The Couriers₀₂
# Dirtbike Manifesto

### STORY: BRIAN WOOD
### ART AND SFX: ROB G
### LETTERS: RYAN YOUNT

**PRODUCED BY AIT/PLANETLAR**
**SAN FRANCISCO**

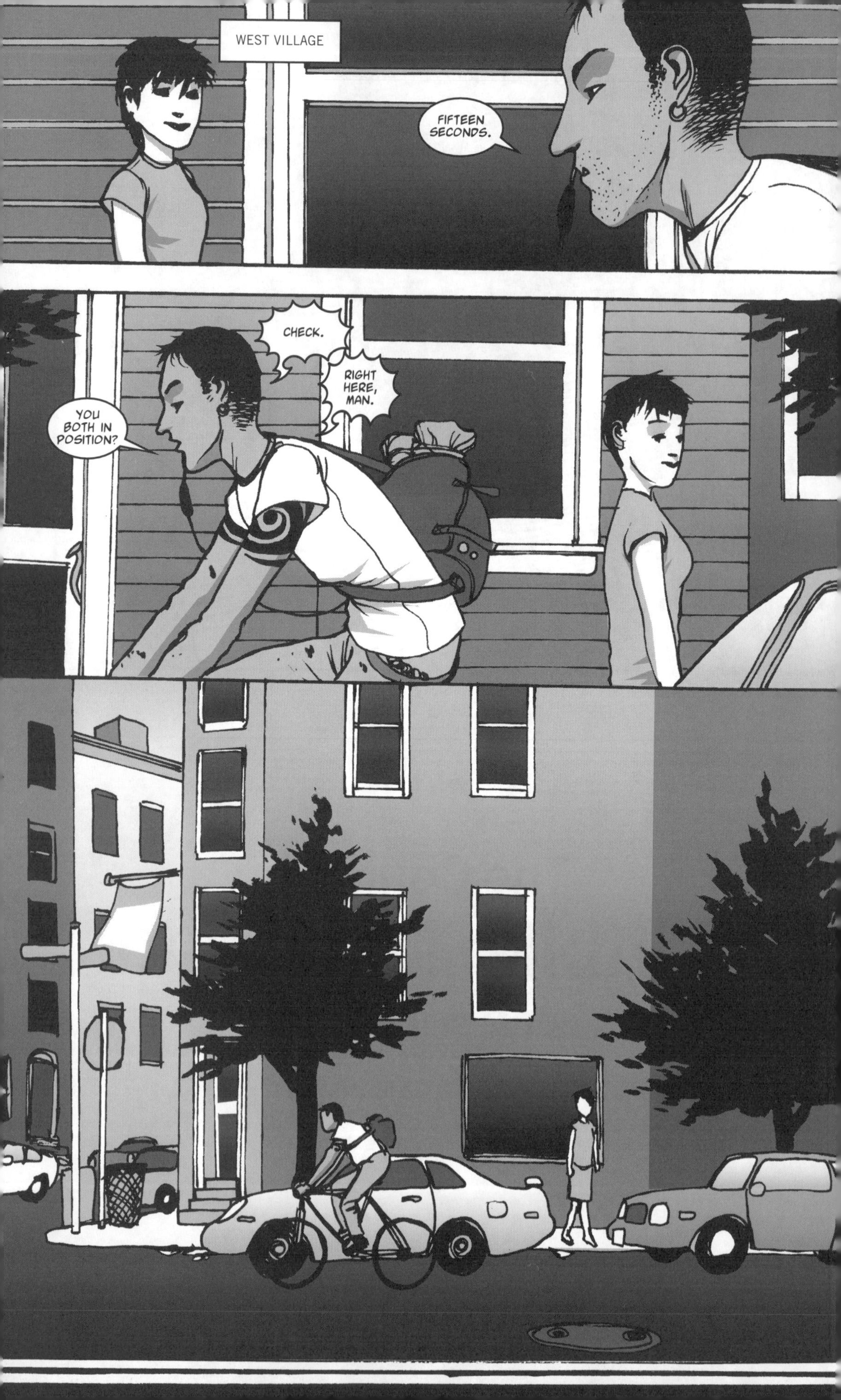
WEST VILLAGE
FIFTEEN SECONDS.
YOU BOTH IN POSITION?
CHECK.
RIGHT HERE, MAN.

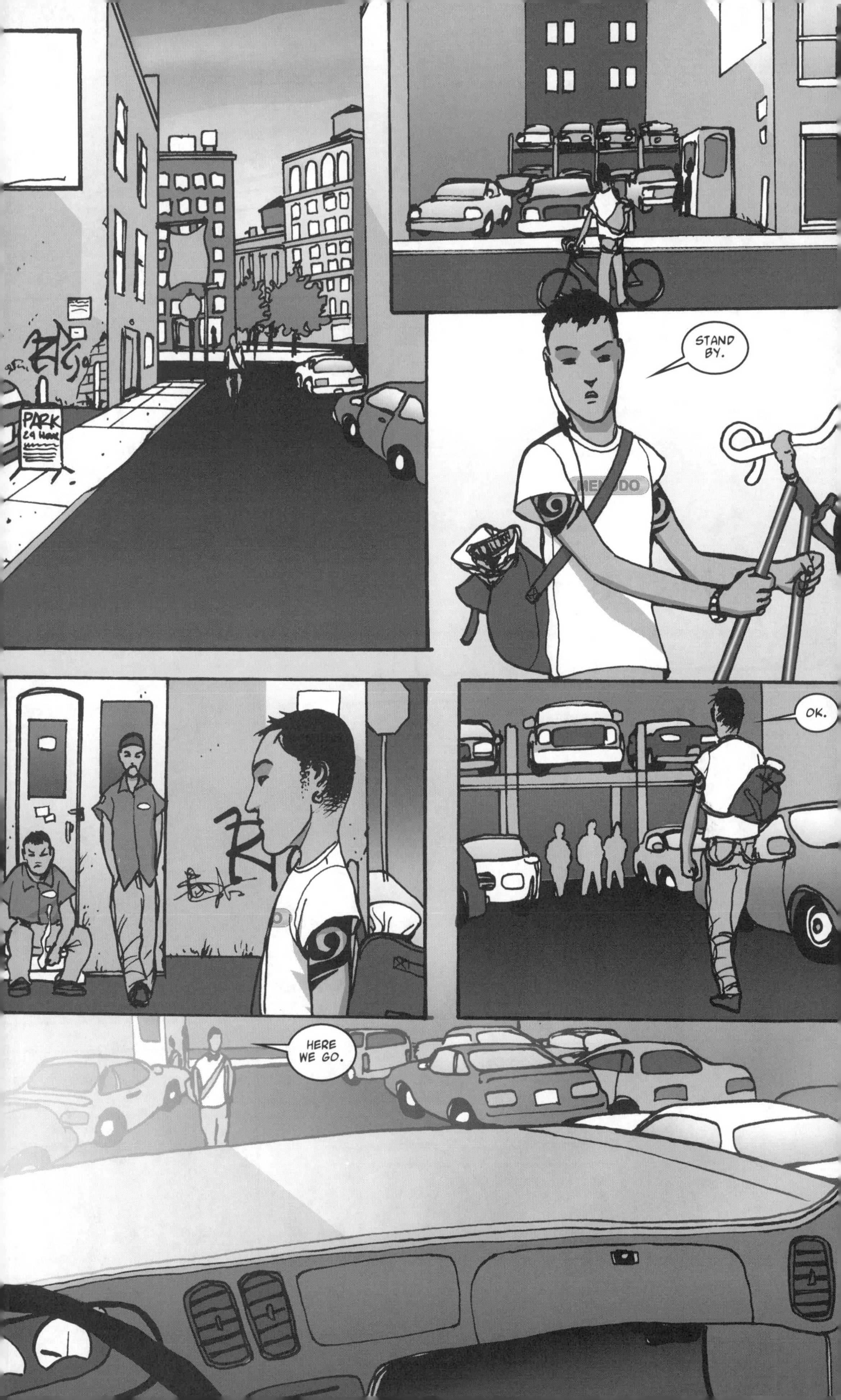
PARK
24 Hour
STAND BY.
OK.
HERE WE GO.

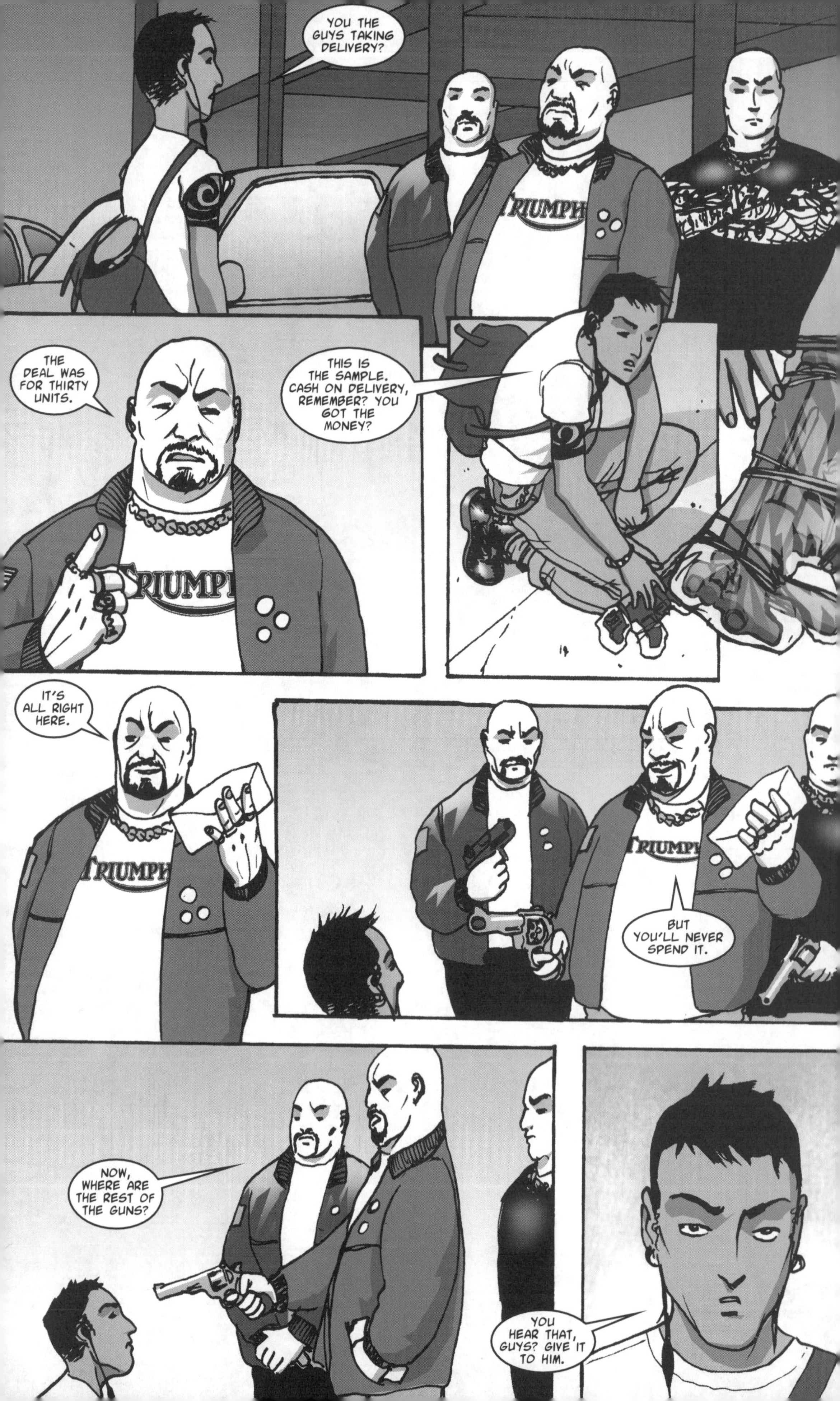
YOU THE GUYS TAKING DELIVERY?
TRIUMPH
THE DEAL WAS FOR THIRTY UNITS.
THIS IS THE SAMPLE. CASH ON DELIVERY, REMEMBER? YOU GOT THE MONEY?
TRIUMPH
IT'S ALL RIGHT HERE.
TRIUMPH
TRIUMPH
BUT YOU'LL NEVER SPEND IT.
NOW, WHERE ARE THE REST OF THE GUNS?
YOU HEAR THAT, GUYS? GIVE IT TO HIM.

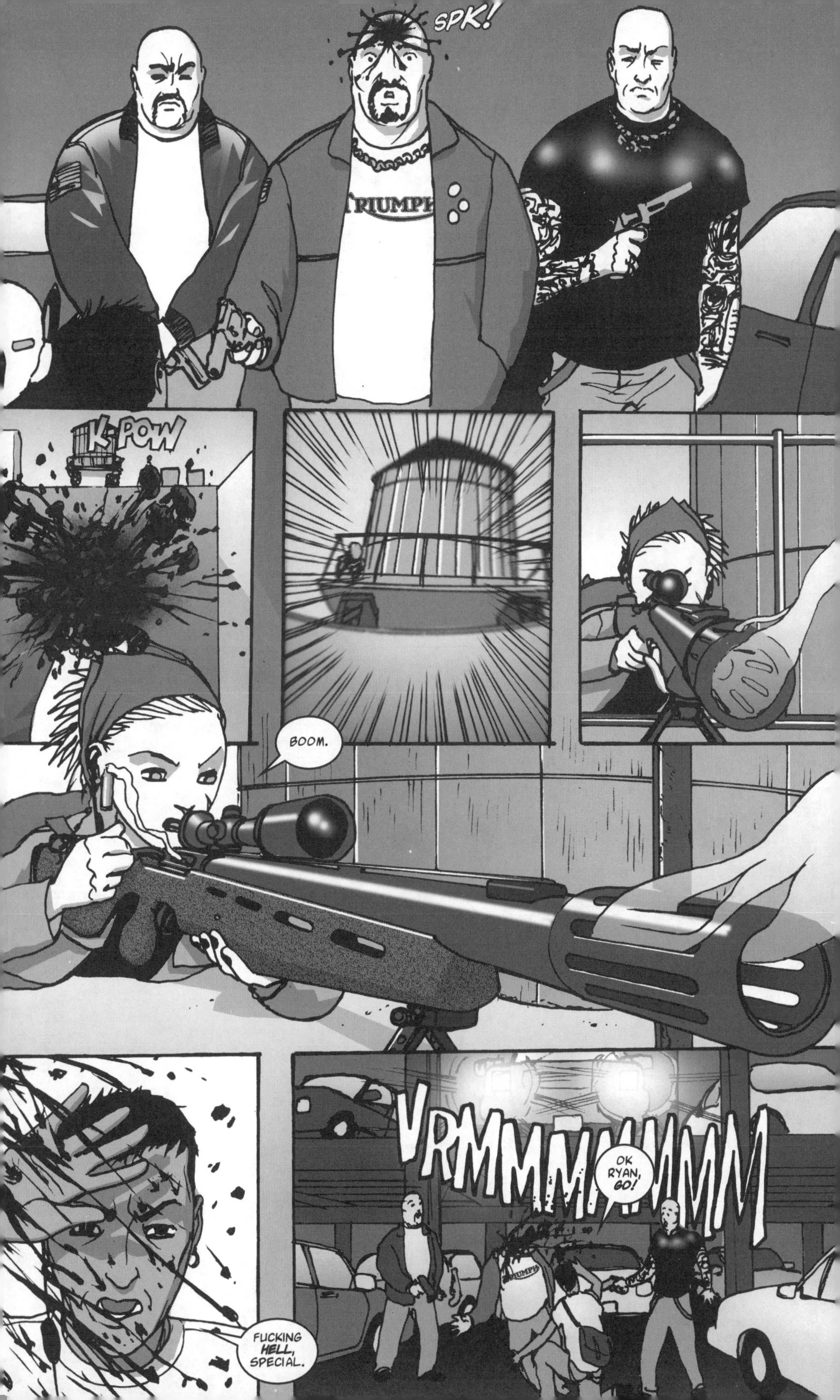
SPK!
TRIUMPH
K-POW
BOOM.
FUCKING HELL, SPECIAL.
VRMMMMMMMM
OK RYAN, GO!

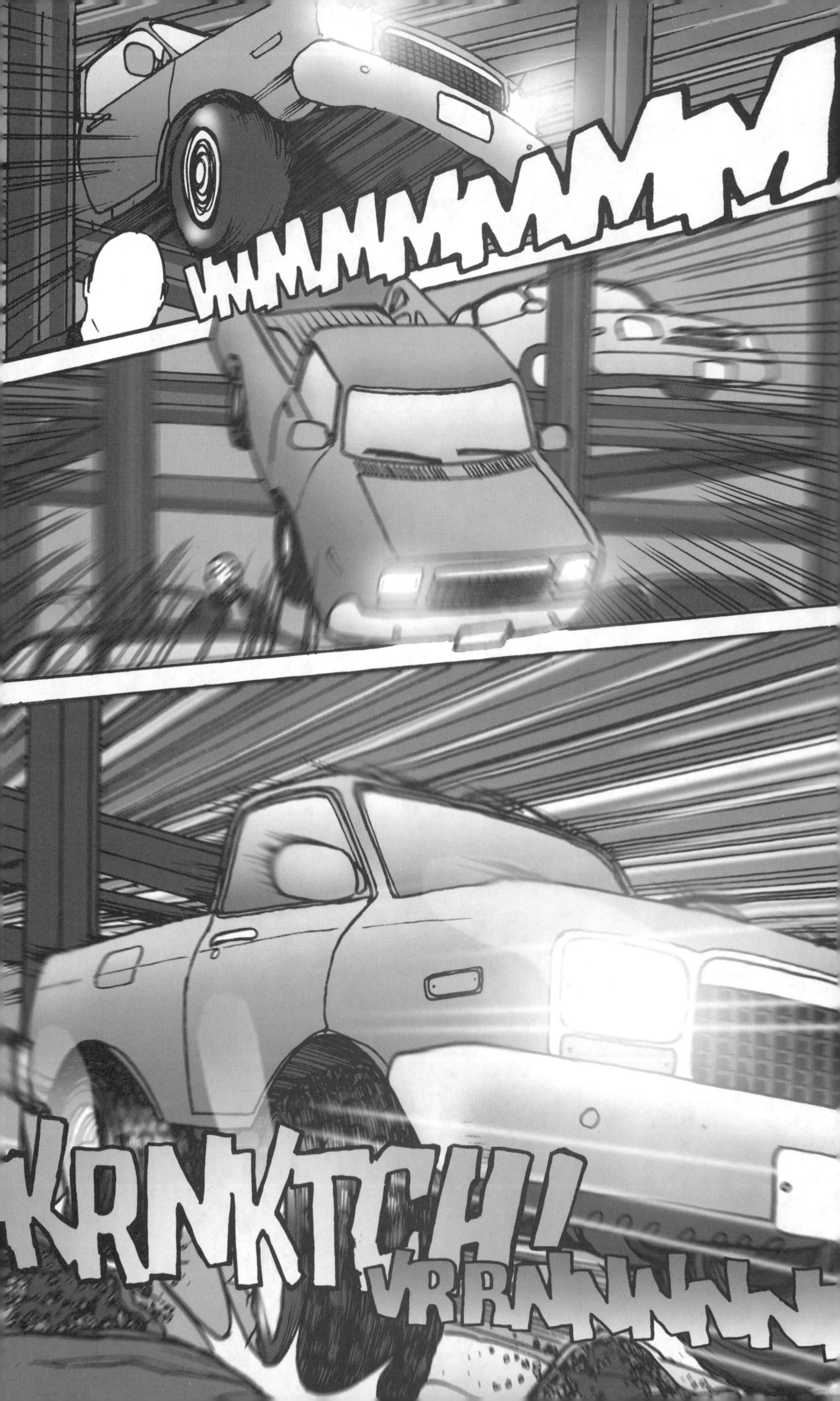
VMMMMMAAAMMM
KRNKTCH!
VRRAAANNN

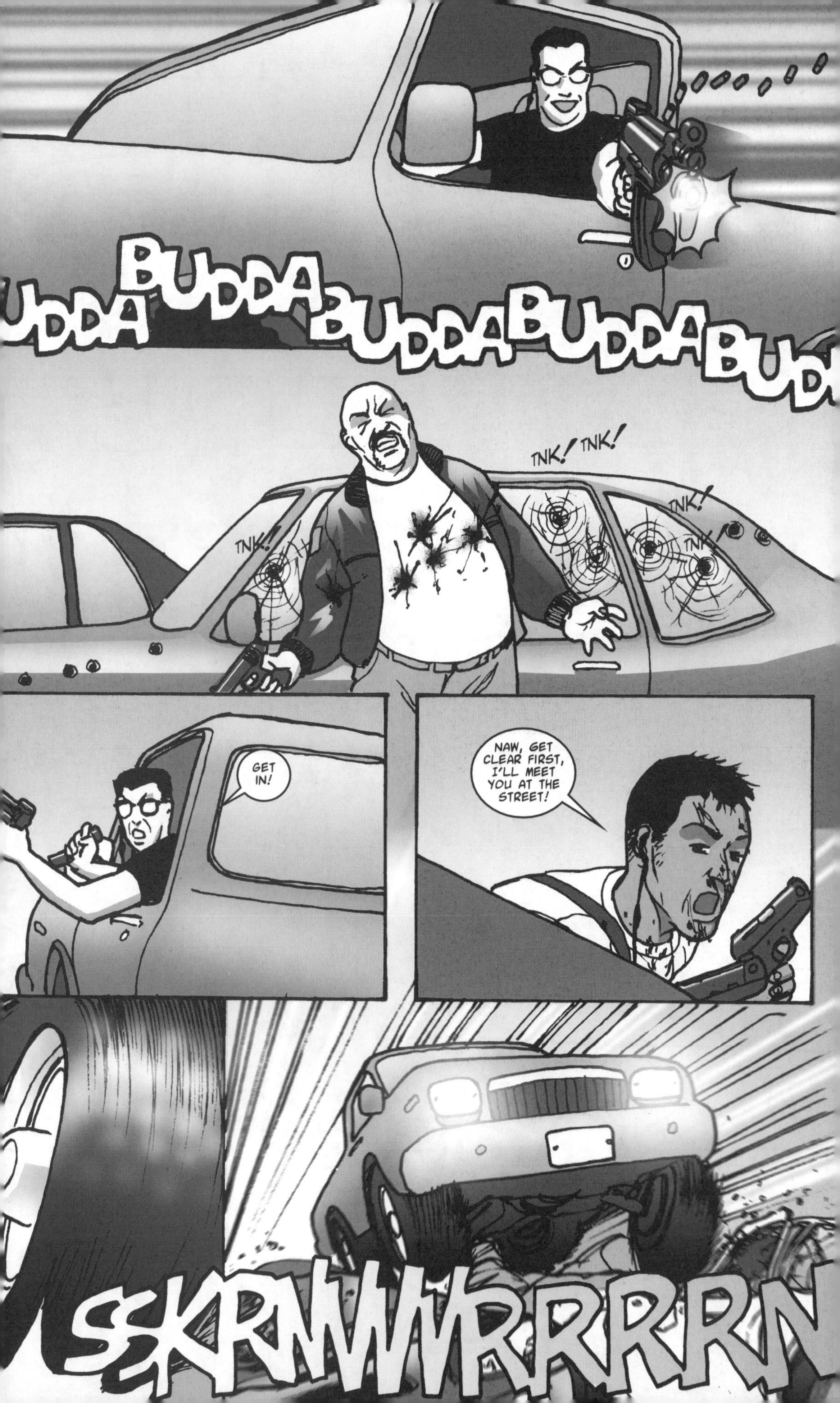
UDDA BUDDA BUDDA BUDDA BUD
TNK! TNK!
TNK!
TNK!
TNK!
GET IN!
NAW, GET CLEAR FIRST, I'LL MEET YOU AT THE STREET!
SKRNNWRRRRN

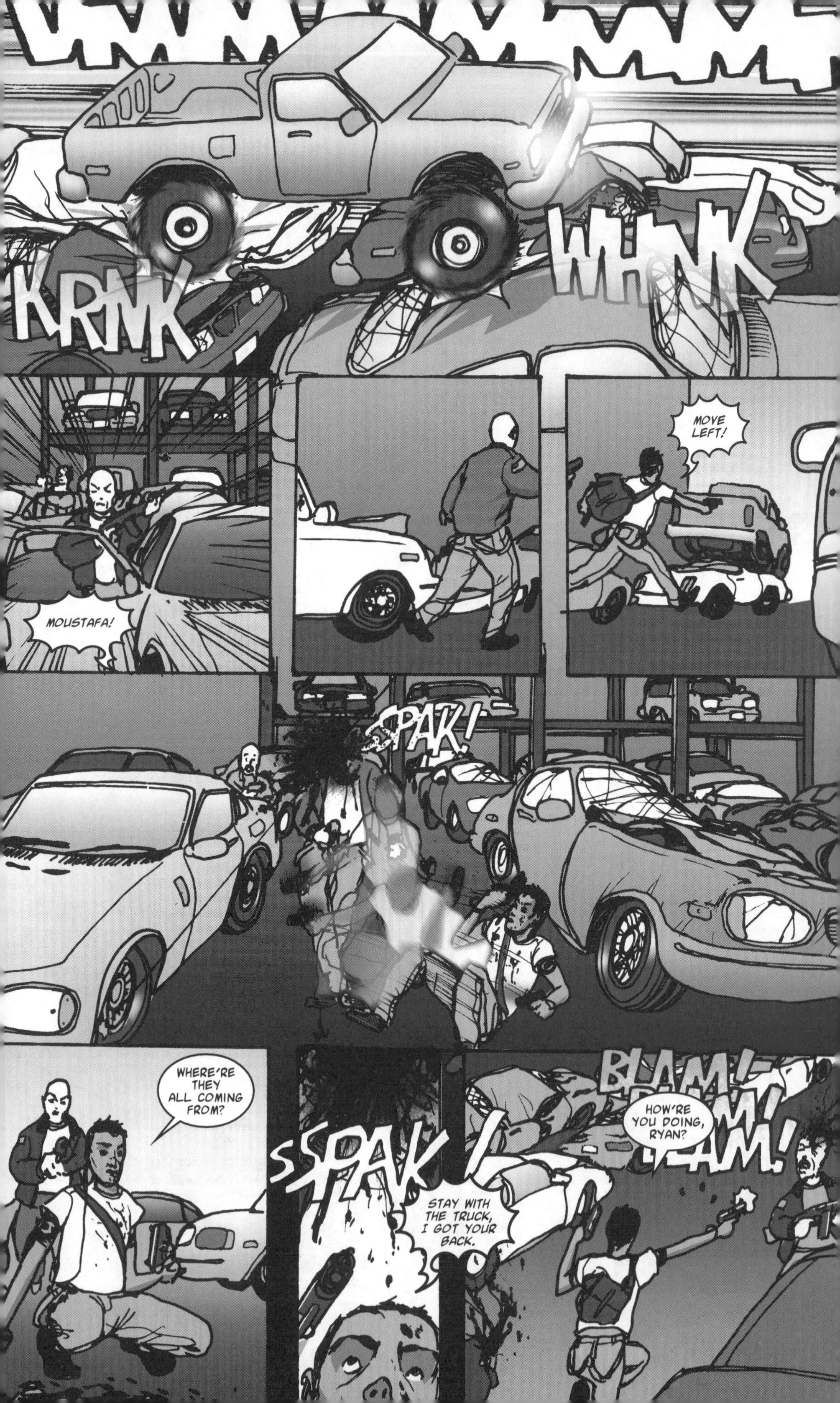
KRINK
WHNK
MOUSTAFA!
MOVE LEFT!
SPAK!
WHERE'RE THEY ALL COMING FROM?
SSPAK!
STAY WITH THE TRUCK, I GOT YOUR BACK.
BLAM!
HOW'RE YOU DOING, RYAN?

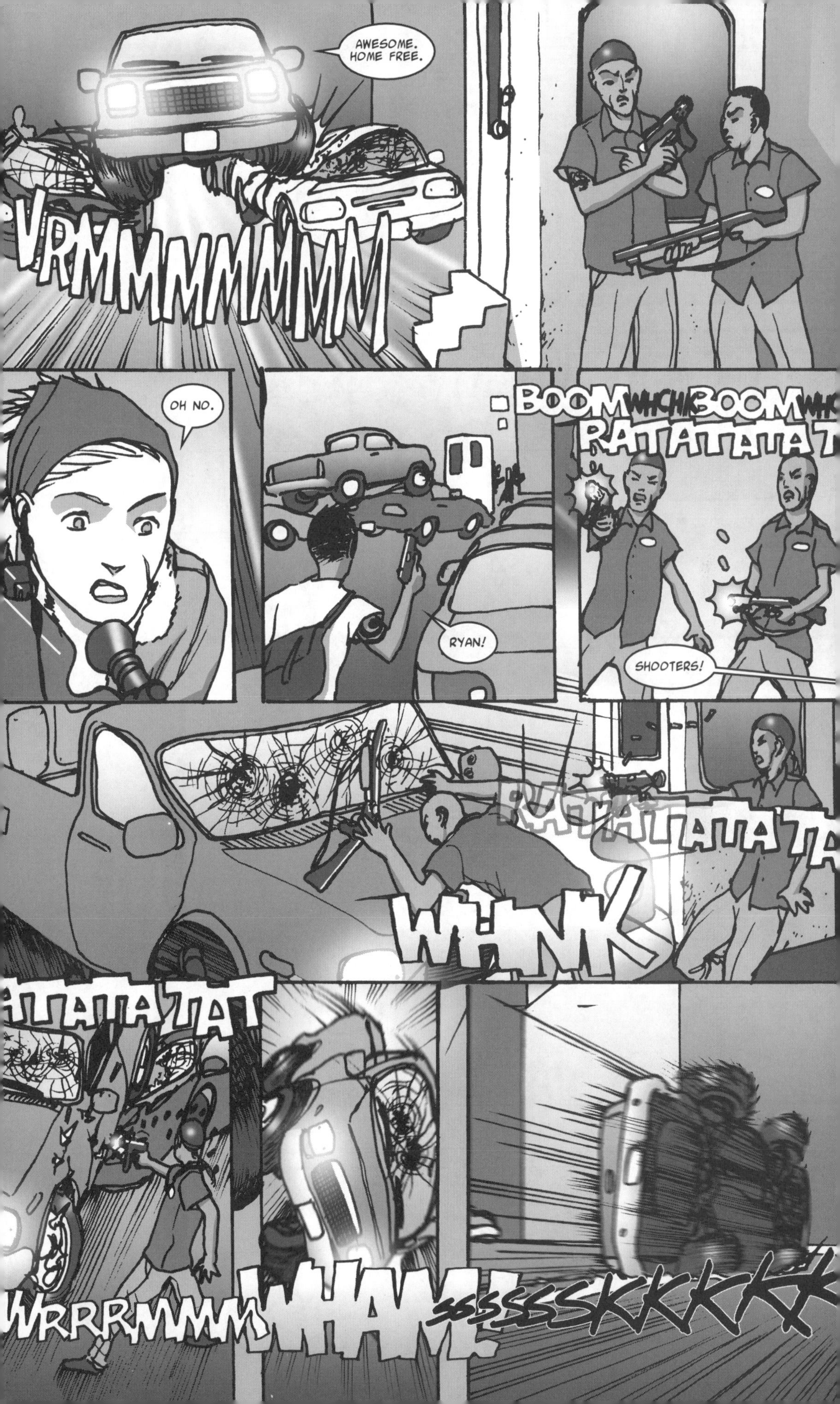
AWESOME. HOME FREE.
VRMMMMMMMM
OH NO.
BOOM WHCHK BOOM
RATATATATA TAT
RYAN!
SHOOTERS!
RATATATATA TAT
WHNK
TATATA TAT
WRRRMMMM
WHAM!
SSSSSSKKKKK

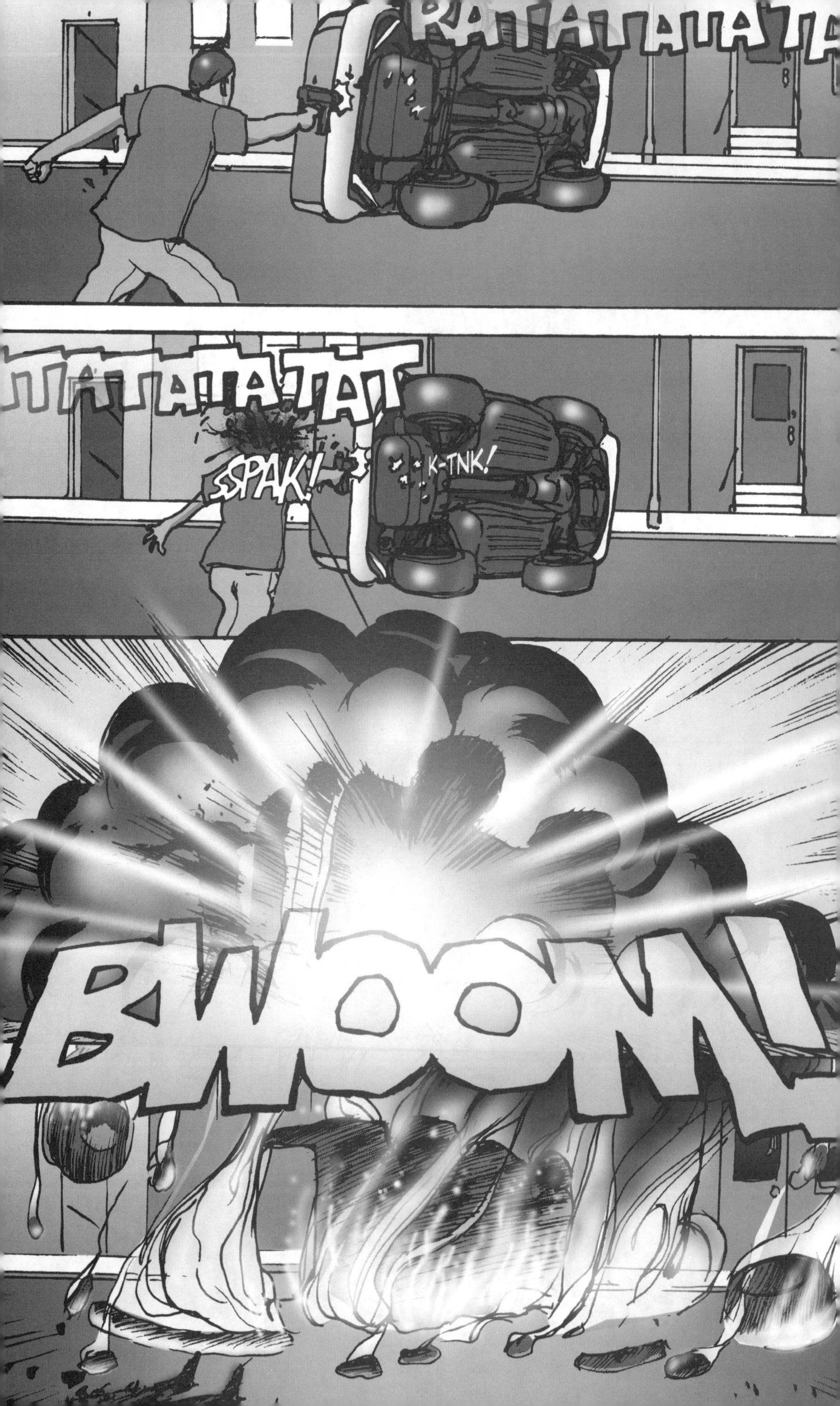
RATATATATA
TATATATAT
SSPAK!
K-TNK!
BWOOM!

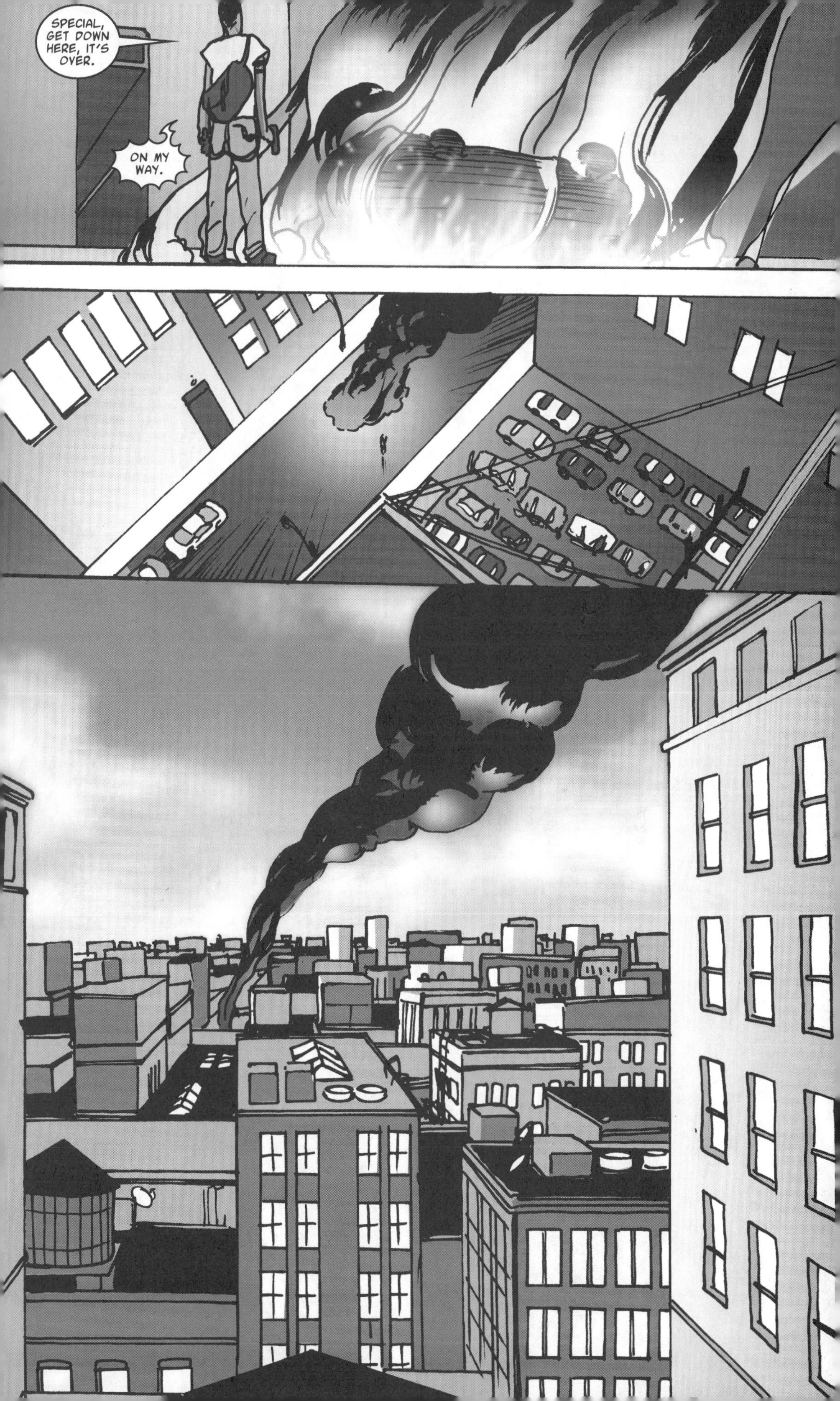
SPECIAL, GET DOWN HERE, IT'S OVER.
ON MY WAY.

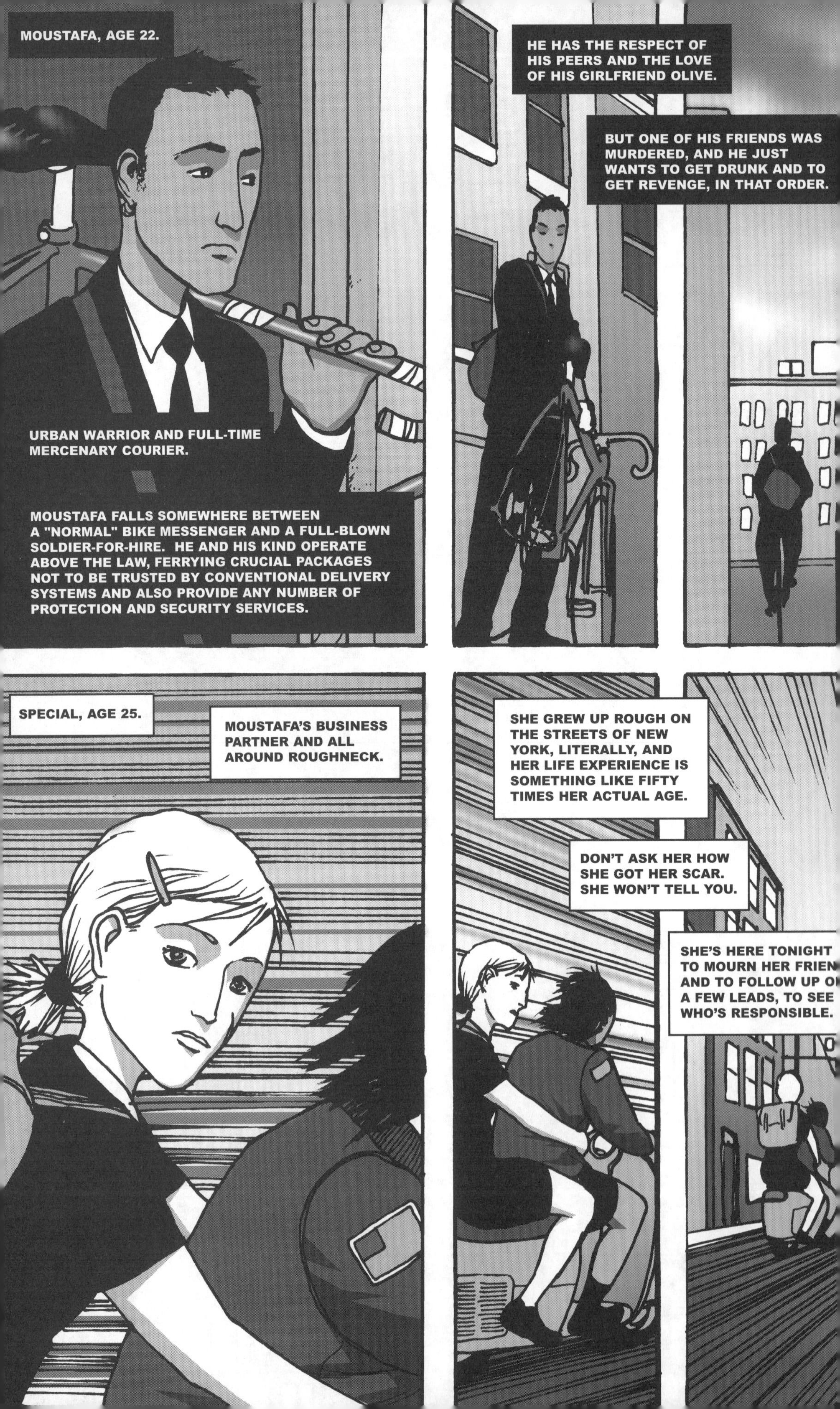
MOUSTAFA, AGE 22.
URBAN WARRIOR AND FULL-TIME MERCENARY COURIER.
MOUSTAFA FALLS SOMEWHERE BETWEEN A "NORMAL" BIKE MESSENGER AND A FULL-BLOWN SOLDIER-FOR-HIRE. HE AND HIS KIND OPERATE ABOVE THE LAW, FERRYING CRUCIAL PACKAGES NOT TO BE TRUSTED BY CONVENTIONAL DELIVERY SYSTEMS AND ALSO PROVIDE ANY NUMBER OF PROTECTION AND SECURITY SERVICES.
HE HAS THE RESPECT OF HIS PEERS AND THE LOVE OF HIS GIRLFRIEND OLIVE.
BUT ONE OF HIS FRIENDS WAS MURDERED, AND HE JUST WANTS TO GET DRUNK AND TO GET REVENGE, IN THAT ORDER.
SPECIAL, AGE 25.
MOUSTAFA'S BUSINESS PARTNER AND ALL AROUND ROUGHNECK.
SHE GREW UP ROUGH ON THE STREETS OF NEW YORK, LITERALLY, AND HER LIFE EXPERIENCE IS SOMETHING LIKE FIFTY TIMES HER ACTUAL AGE.
DON'T ASK HER HOW SHE GOT HER SCAR. SHE WON'T TELL YOU.
SHE'S HERE TONIGHT TO MOURN HER FRIEN AND TO FOLLOW UP O A FEW LEADS, TO SEE WHO'S RESPONSIBLE.

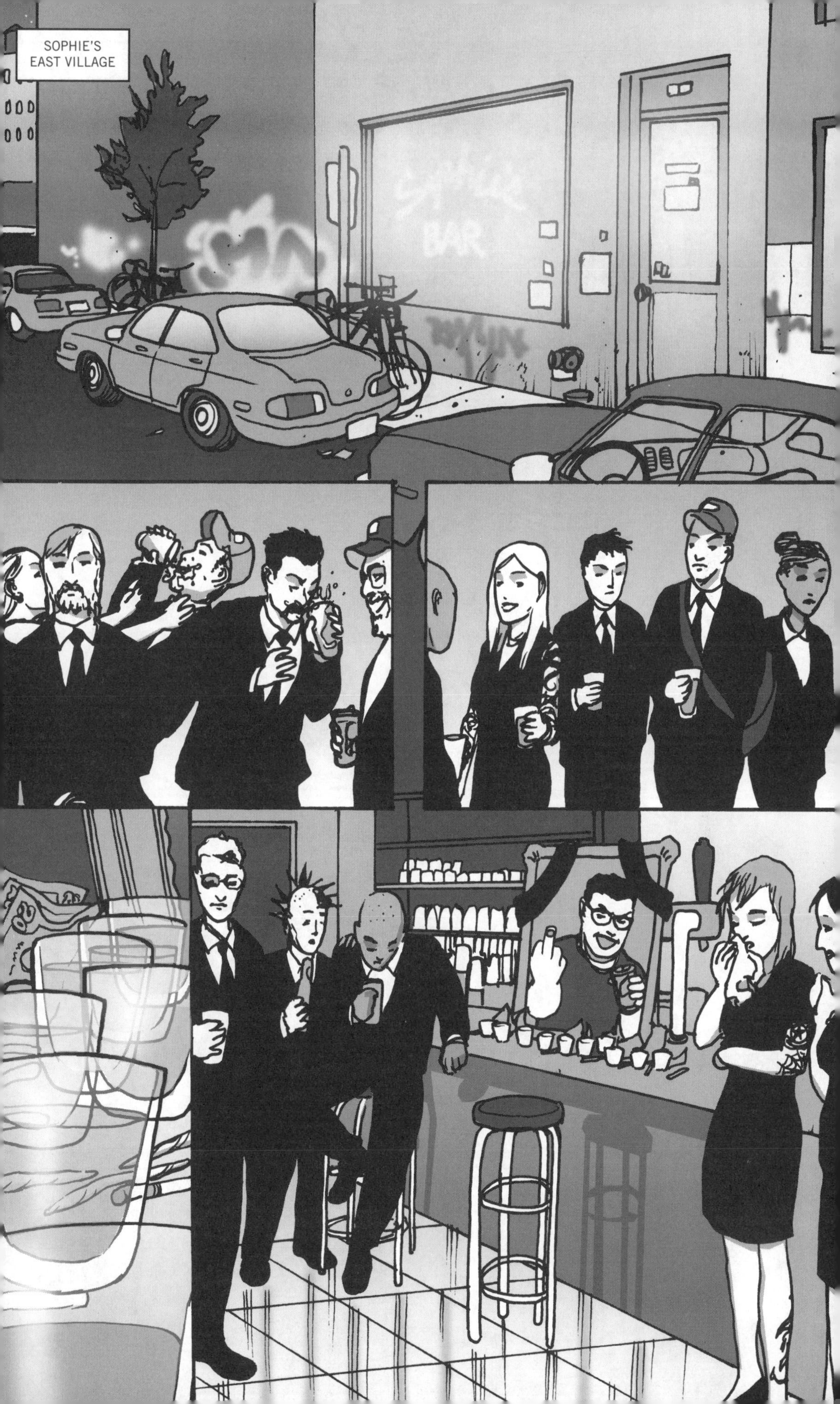
SOPHIE'S
EAST VILLAGE
BAR

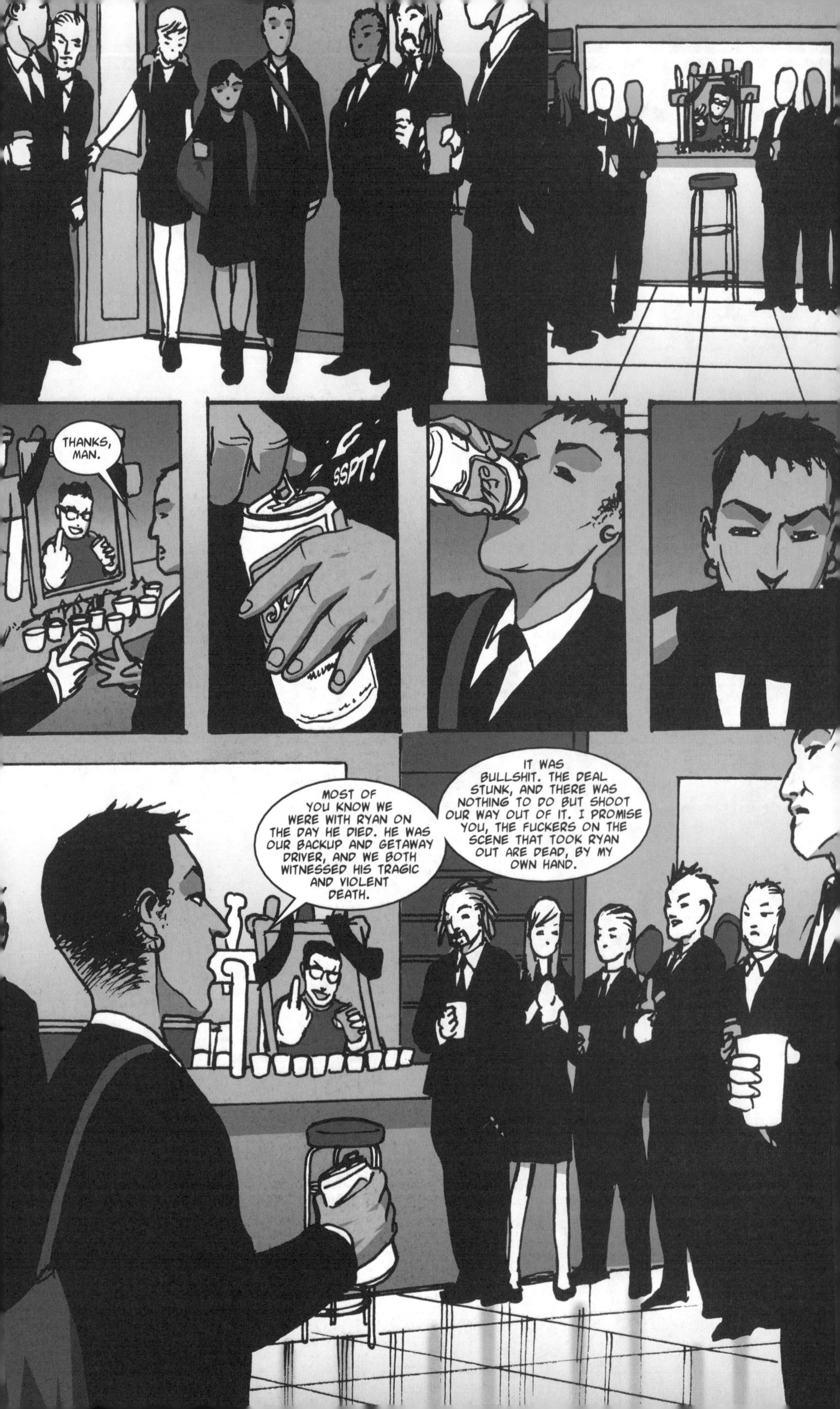
THANKS, MAN.
SSPT!
MOST OF YOU KNOW WE WERE WITH RYAN ON THE DAY HE DIED. HE WAS OUR BACKUP AND GETAWAY DRIVER, AND WE BOTH WITNESSED HIS TRAGIC AND VIOLENT DEATH.
IT WAS BULLSHIT. THE DEAL STUNK, AND THERE WAS NOTHING TO DO BUT SHOOT OUR WAY OUT OF IT. I PROMISE YOU, THE FUCKERS ON THE SCENE THAT TOOK RYAN OUT ARE DEAD, BY MY OWN HAND.

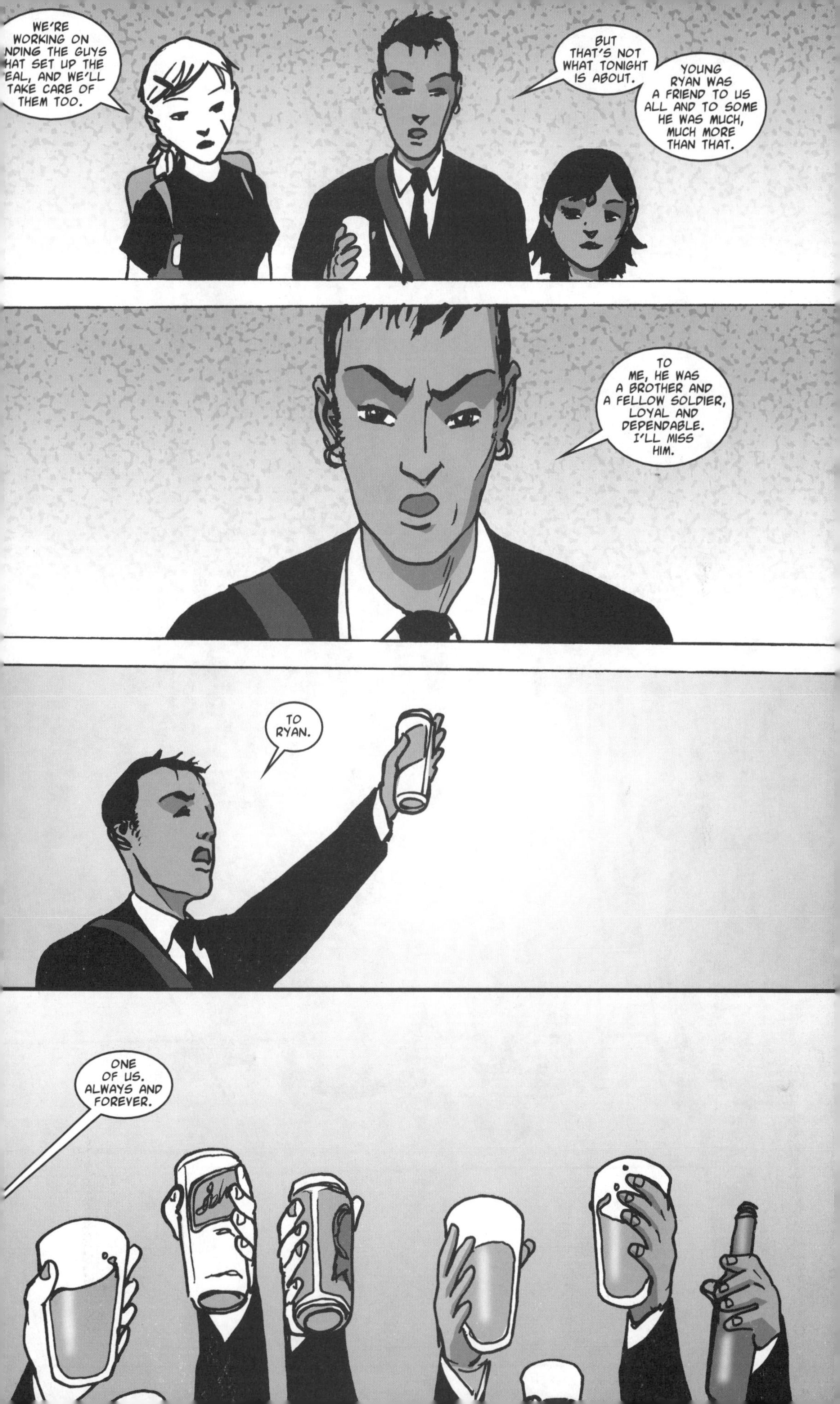
WE'RE WORKING ON NDING THE GUYS HAT SET UP THE EAL, AND WE'LL TAKE CARE OF THEM TOO.
BUT THAT'S NOT WHAT TONIGHT IS ABOUT.
YOUNG RYAN WAS A FRIEND TO US ALL AND TO SOME HE WAS MUCH, MUCH MORE THAN THAT.
TO ME, HE WAS A BROTHER AND A FELLOW SOLDIER, LOYAL AND DEPENDABLE. I'LL MISS HIM.
TO RYAN.
ONE OF US. ALWAYS AND FOREVER.

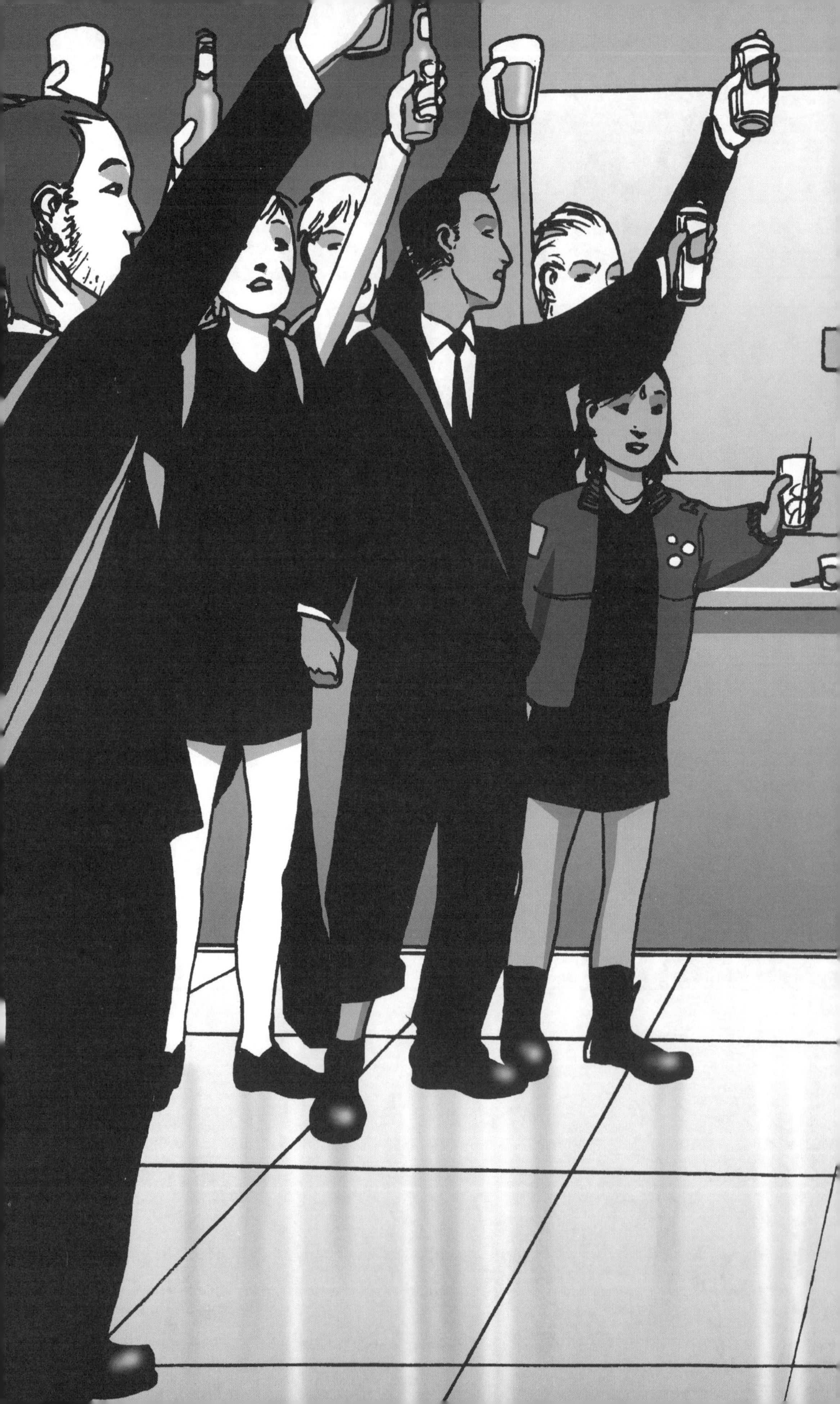

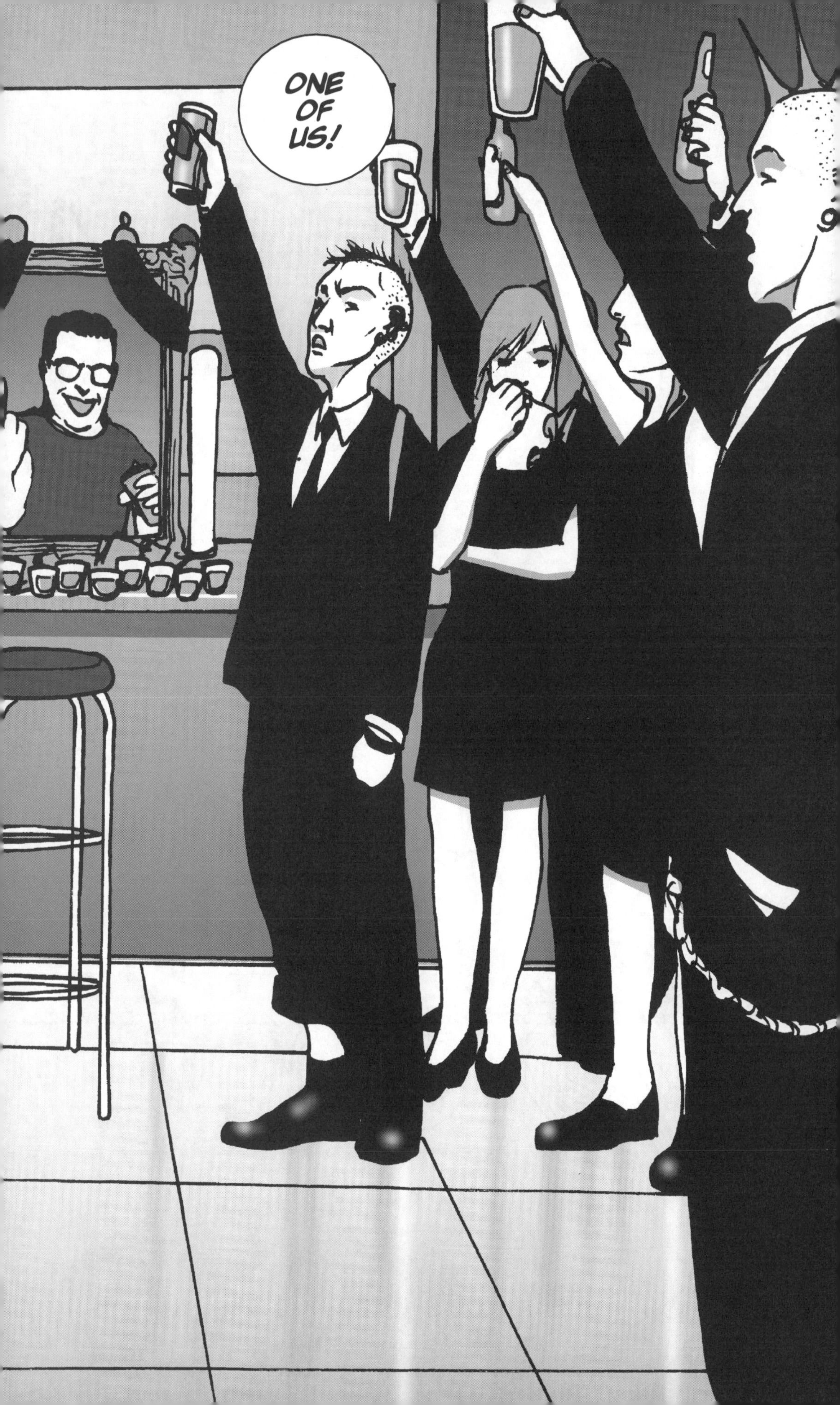
ONE OF US!

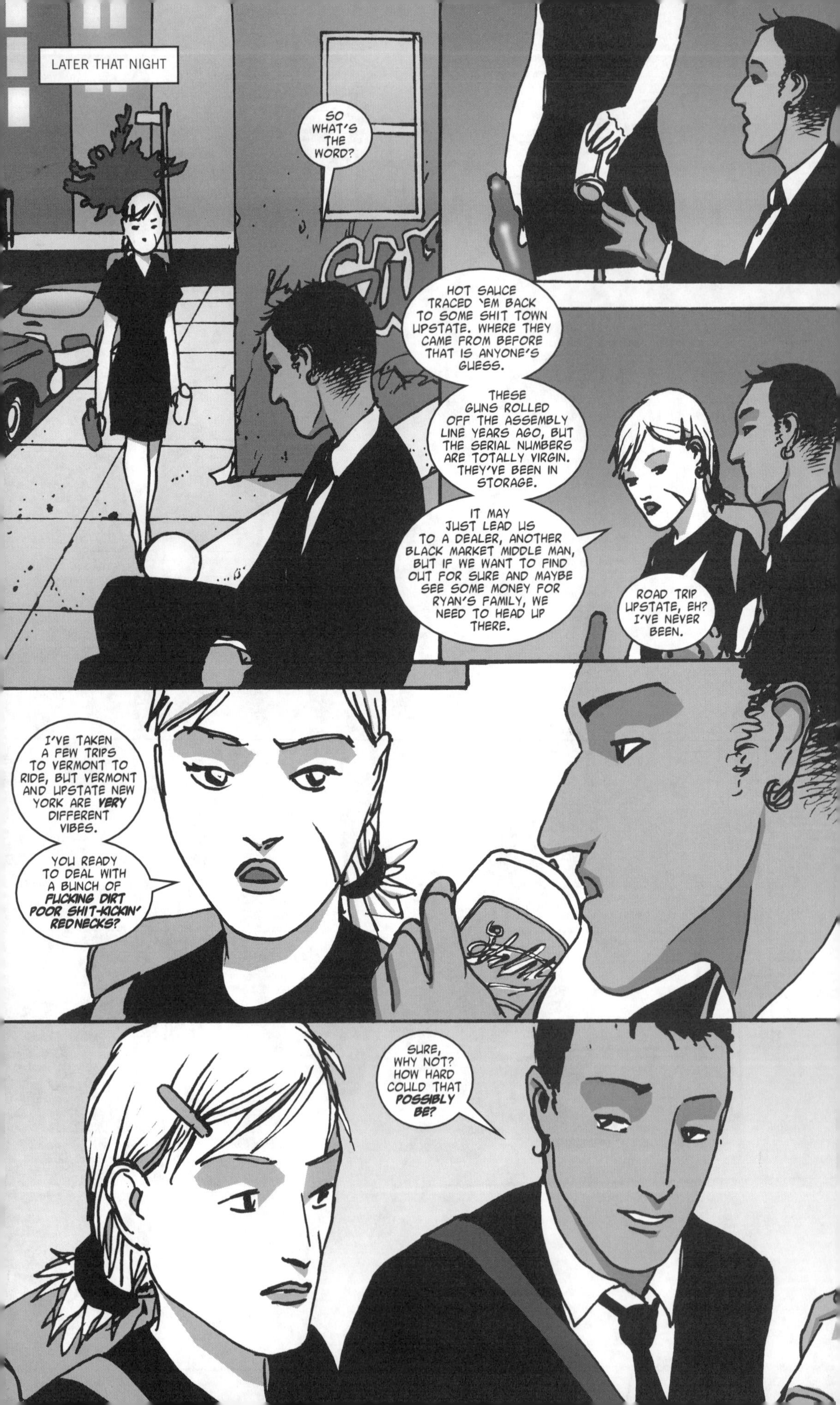

LATER THAT NIGHT
SO WHAT'S THE WORD?
HOT SAUCE TRACED 'EM BACK TO SOME SHIT TOWN UPSTATE. WHERE THEY CAME FROM BEFORE THAT IS ANYONE'S GUESS.
THESE GUNS ROLLED OFF THE ASSEMBLY LINE YEARS AGO, BUT THE SERIAL NUMBERS ARE TOTALLY VIRGIN. THEY'VE BEEN IN STORAGE.
IT MAY JUST LEAD US TO A DEALER, ANOTHER BLACK MARKET MIDDLE MAN, BUT IF WE WANT TO FIND OUT FOR SURE AND MAYBE SEE SOME MONEY FOR RYAN'S FAMILY, WE NEED TO HEAD UP THERE.
ROAD TRIP UPSTATE, EH? I'VE NEVER BEEN.
I'VE TAKEN A FEW TRIPS TO VERMONT TO RIDE, BUT VERMONT AND UPSTATE NEW YORK ARE **VERY** DIFFERENT VIBES.
YOU READY TO DEAL WITH A BUNCH OF ***FUCKING DIRT POOR SHIT-KICKIN' REDNECKS?***
SURE, WHY NOT? HOW HARD COULD THAT **POSSIBLY BE?**

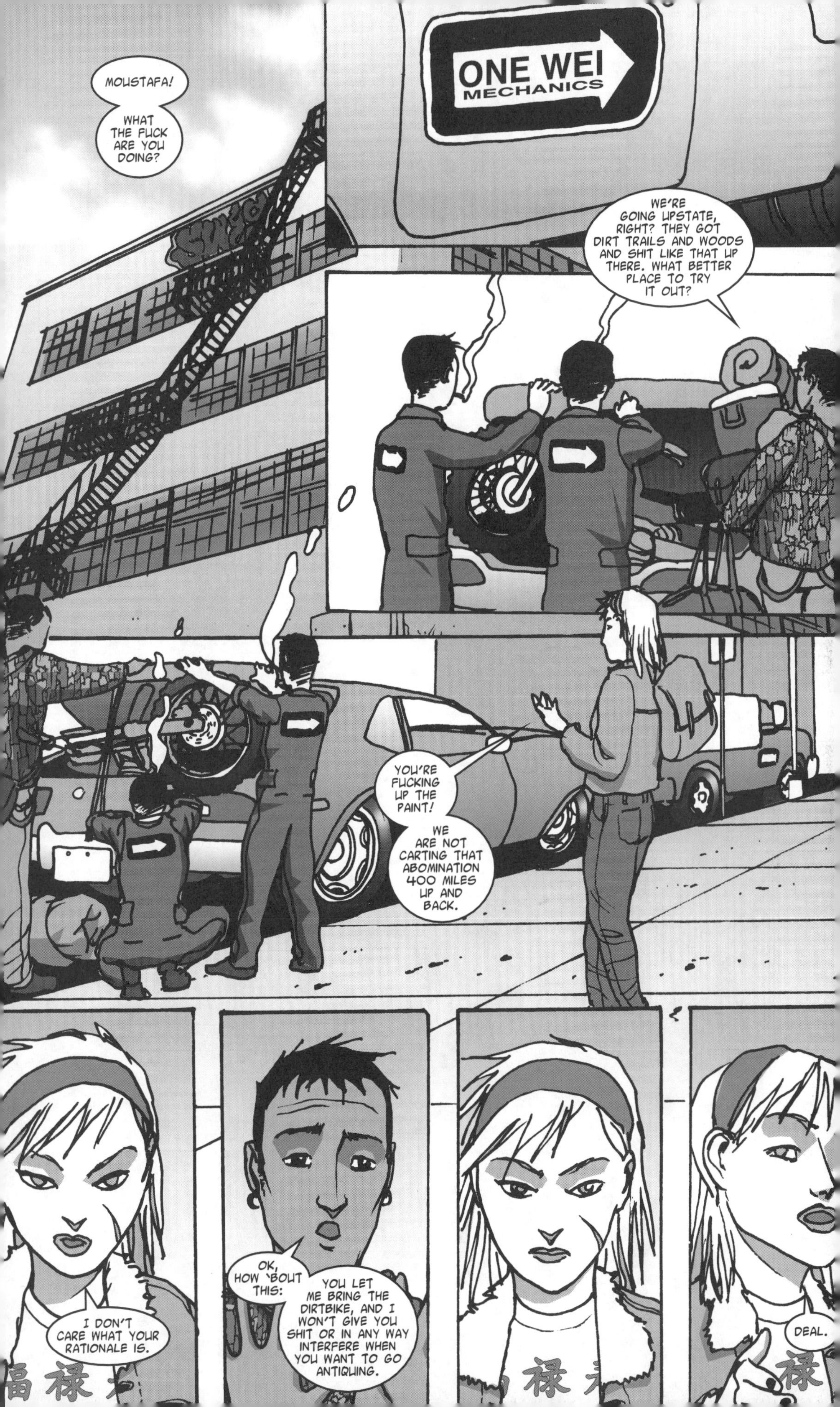
MOUSTAFA!
WHAT THE FUCK ARE YOU DOING?
ONE WEI MECHANICS
WE'RE GOING UPSTATE, RIGHT? THEY GOT DIRT TRAILS AND WOODS AND SHIT LIKE THAT UP THERE. WHAT BETTER PLACE TO TRY IT OUT?
YOU'RE FUCKING UP THE PAINT!
WE ARE NOT CARTING THAT ABOMINATION 400 MILES UP AND BACK.
I DON'T CARE WHAT YOUR RATIONALE IS.
OK, HOW 'BOUT THIS:
YOU LET ME BRING THE DIRTBIKE, AND I WON'T GIVE YOU SHIT OR IN ANY WAY INTERFERE WHEN YOU WANT TO GO ANTIQUING.
DEAL.

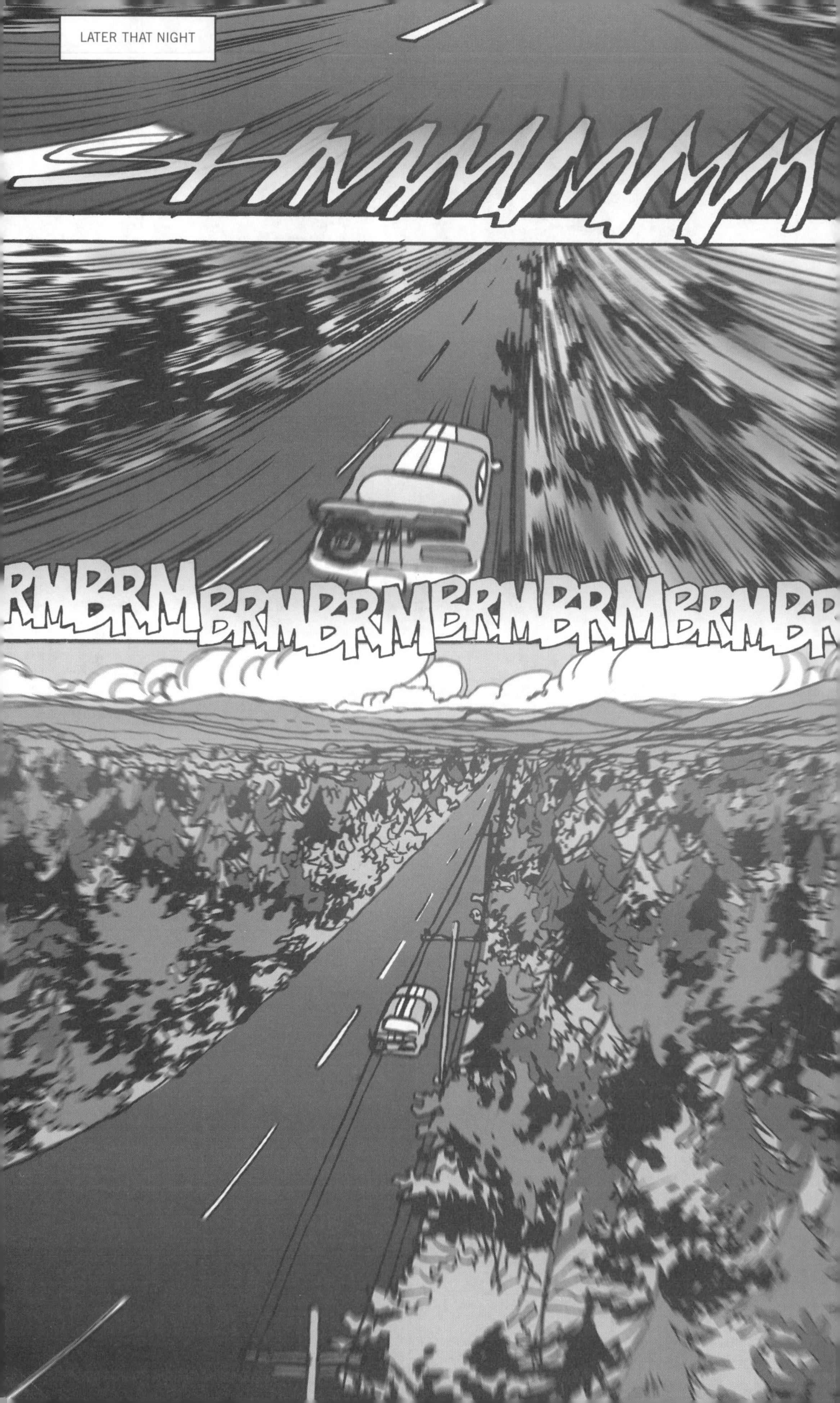
LATER THAT NIGHT
SHMMMMMM
RMBRMBRMBRMBRMBRMBRMBRMBRMBR

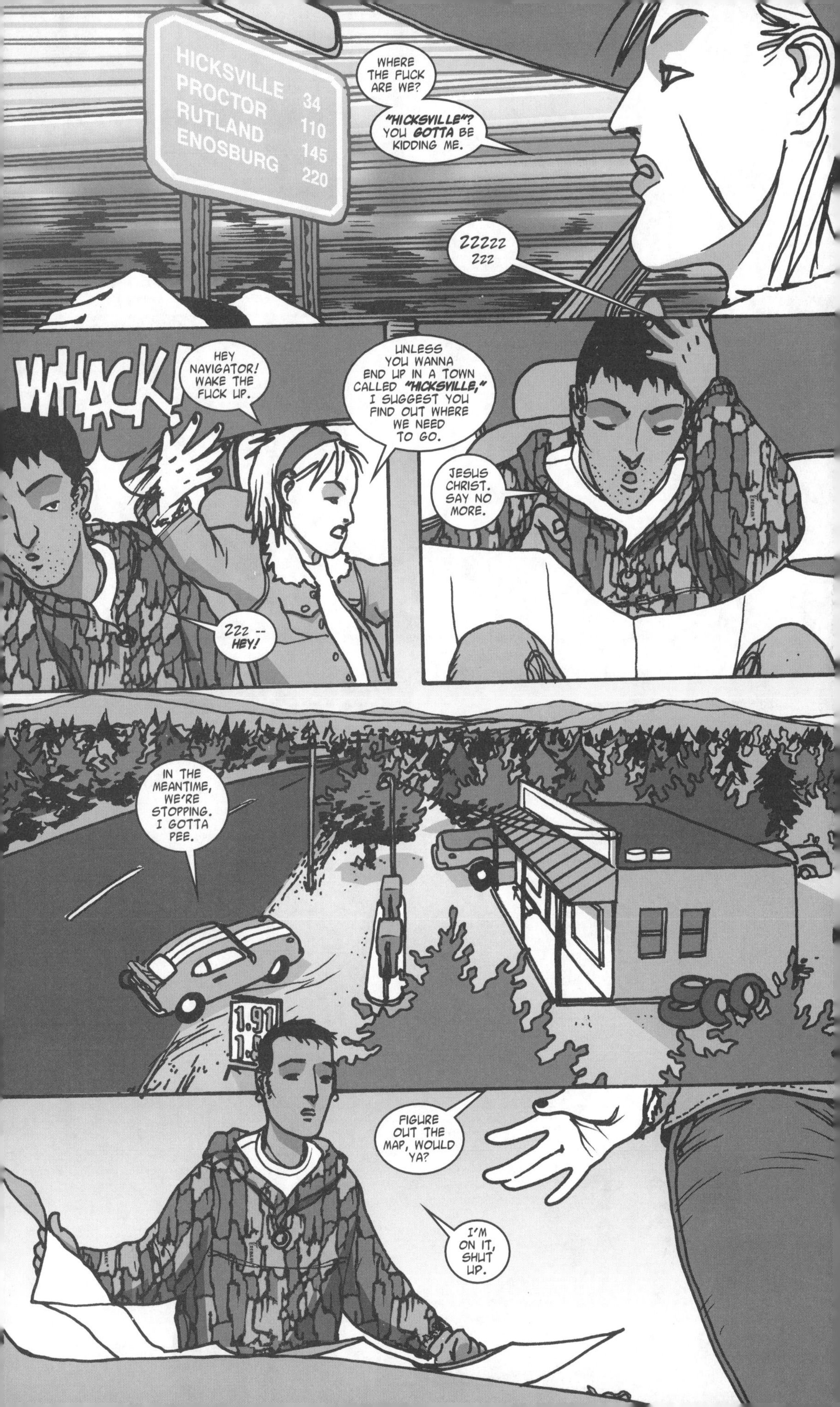
HICKSVILLE 34
PROCTOR 110
RUTLAND 145
ENOSBURG 220
WHERE THE FUCK ARE WE?
"HICKSVILLE"? YOU GOTTA BE KIDDING ME.
ZZZZZ ZZZ
WHACK!
HEY NAVIGATOR! WAKE THE FUCK UP.
UNLESS YOU WANNA END UP IN A TOWN CALLED "HICKSVILLE," I SUGGEST YOU FIND OUT WHERE WE NEED TO GO.
ZZZ -- HEY!
JESUS CHRIST. SAY NO MORE.
IN THE MEANTIME, WE'RE STOPPING. I GOTTA PEE.
FIGURE OUT THE MAP, WOULD YA?
I'M ON IT, SHUT UP.

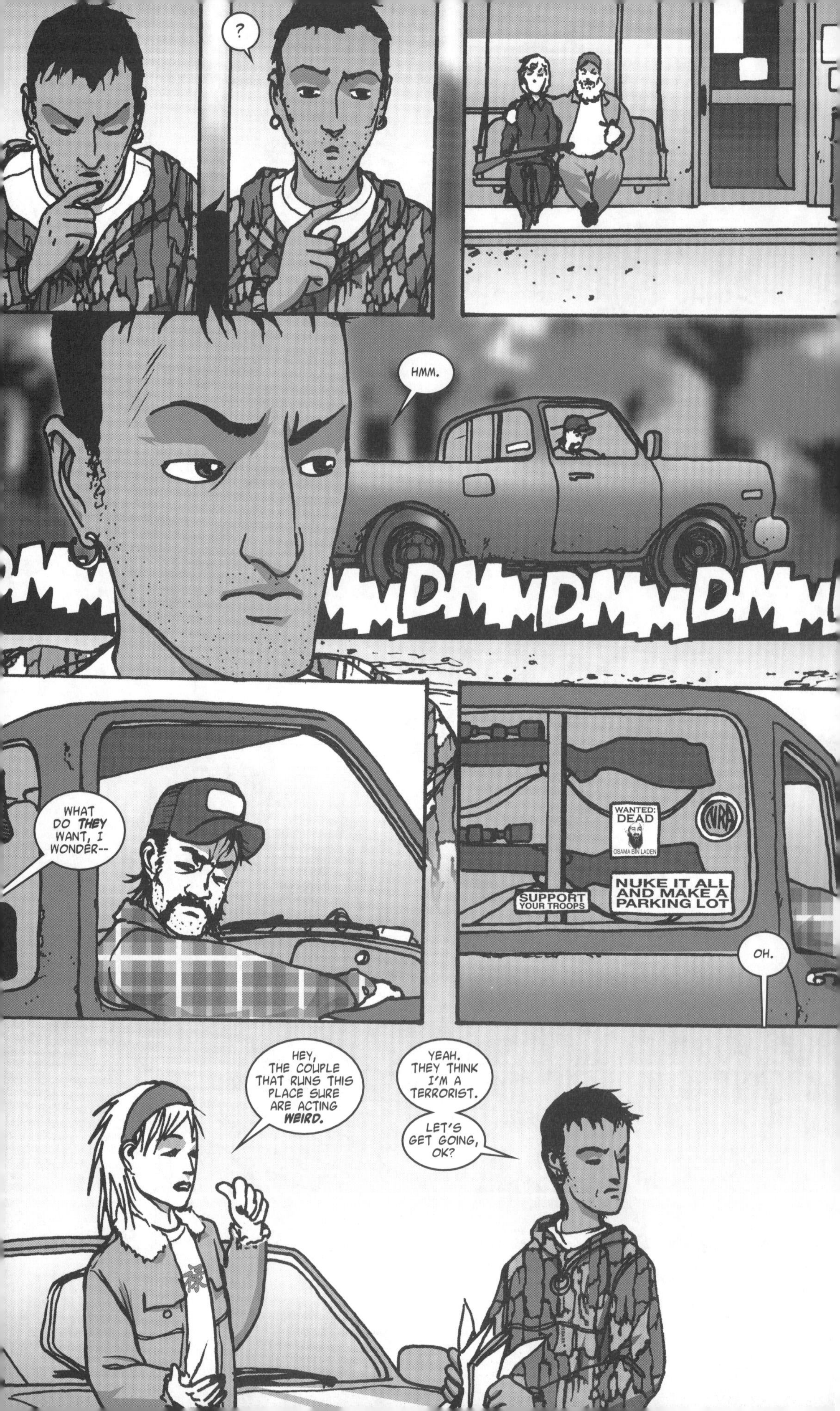
?
HMM.
DMMDMMDMMDMM
WHAT DO THEY WANT, I WONDER--
WANTED: DEAD
OSAMA BIN LADEN
NRA
NUKE IT ALL AND MAKE A PARKING LOT
SUPPORT YOUR TROOPS
OH.
HEY, THE COUPLE THAT RUNS THIS PLACE SURE ARE ACTING WEIRD.
YEAH. THEY THINK I'M A TERRORIST.
LET'S GET GOING, OK?

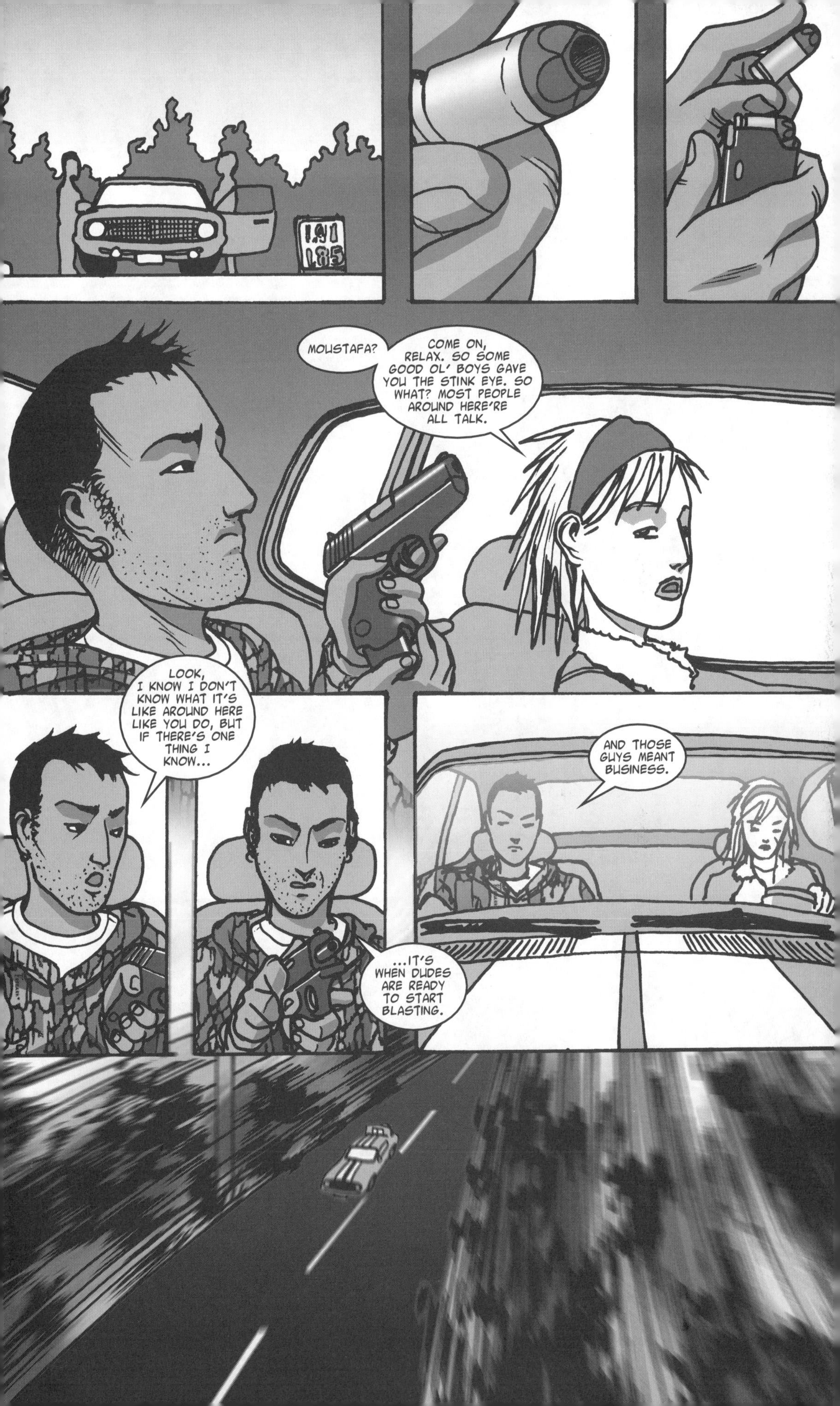

MOUSTAFA?
COME ON, RELAX. SO SOME GOOD OL' BOYS GAVE YOU THE STINK EYE. SO WHAT? MOST PEOPLE AROUND HERE'RE ALL TALK.
LOOK, I KNOW I DON'T KNOW WHAT IT'S LIKE AROUND HERE LIKE YOU DO, BUT IF THERE'S ONE THING I KNOW...
...IT'S WHEN DUDES ARE READY TO START BLASTING.
AND THOSE GUYS MEANT BUSINESS.

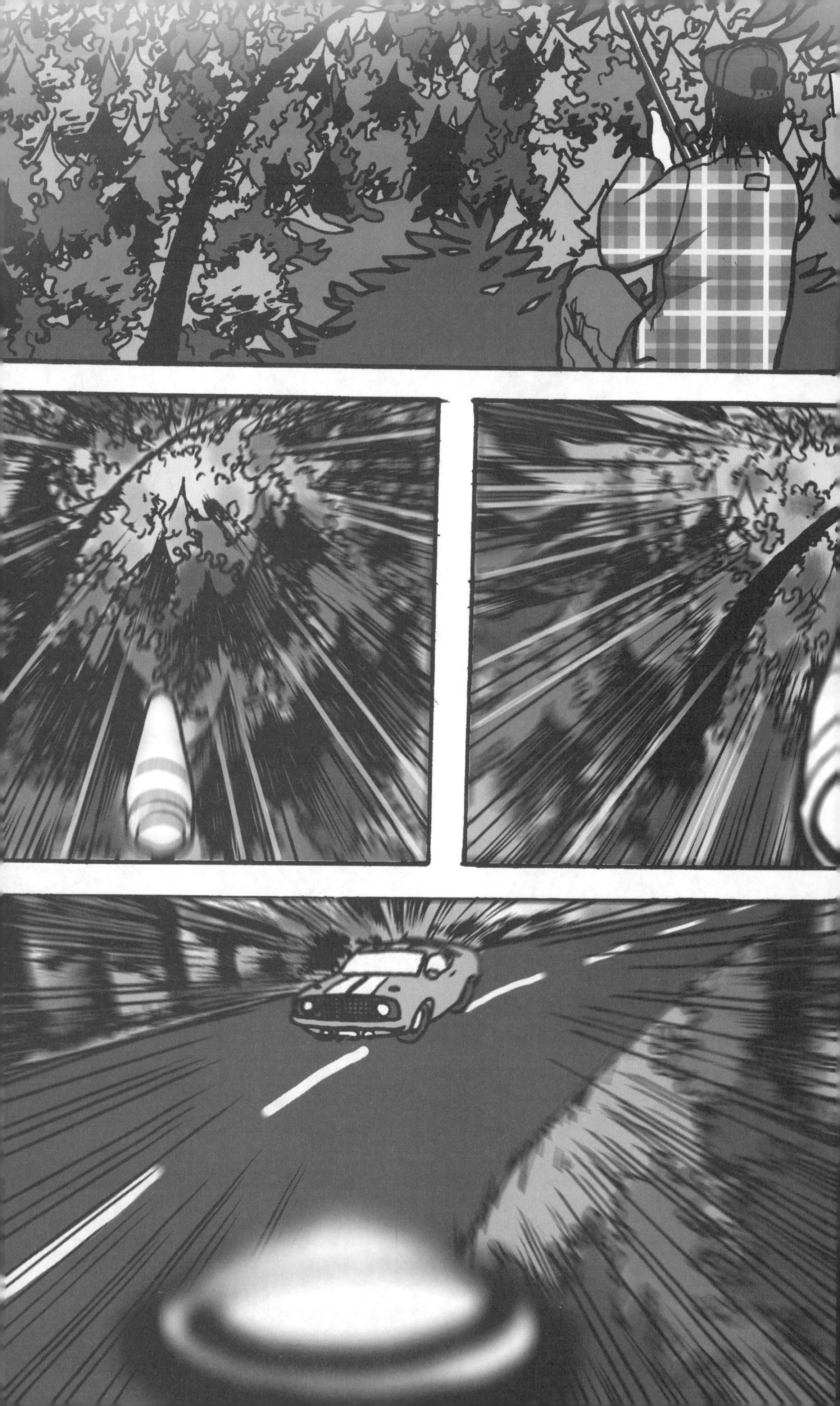

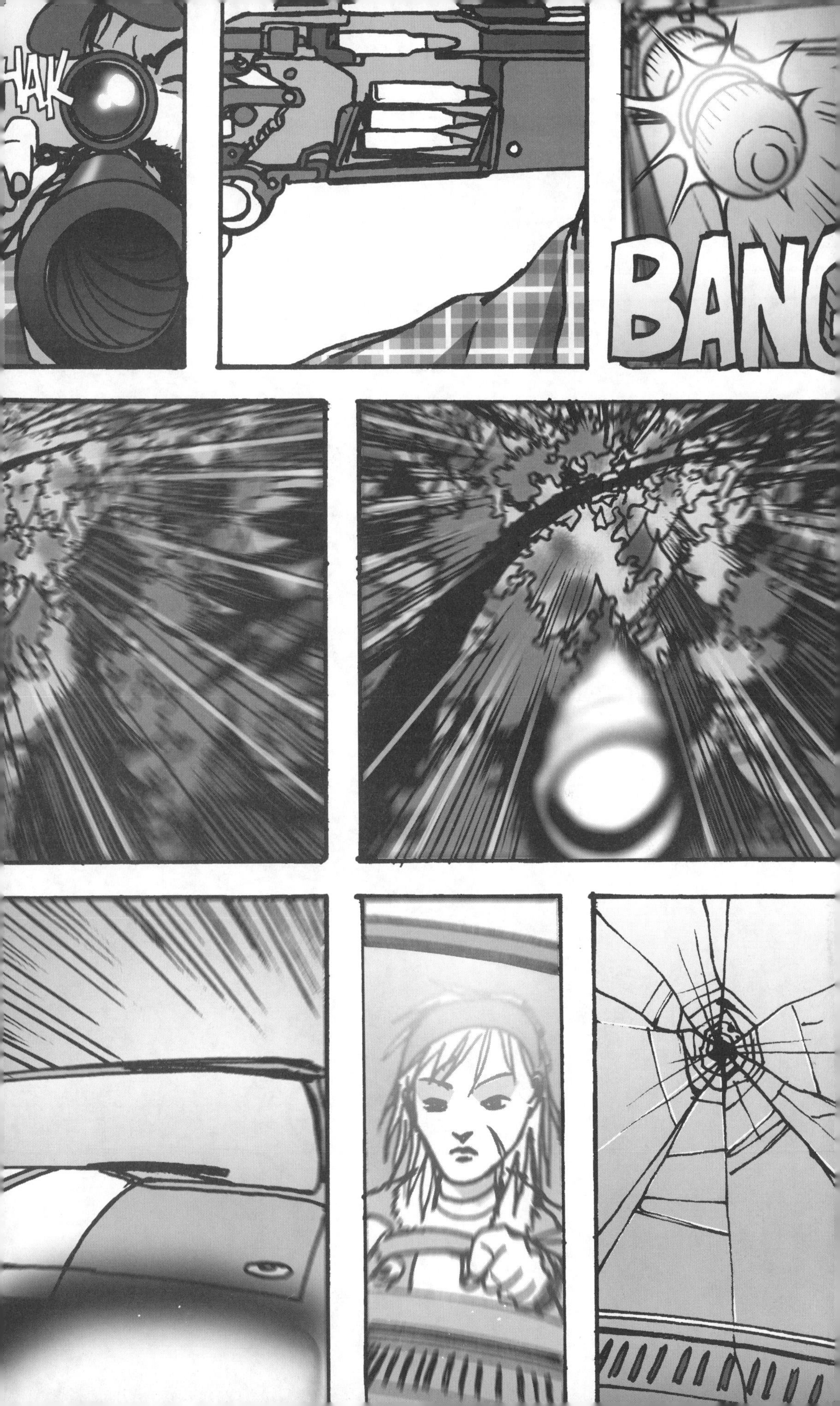
HAK
BAN

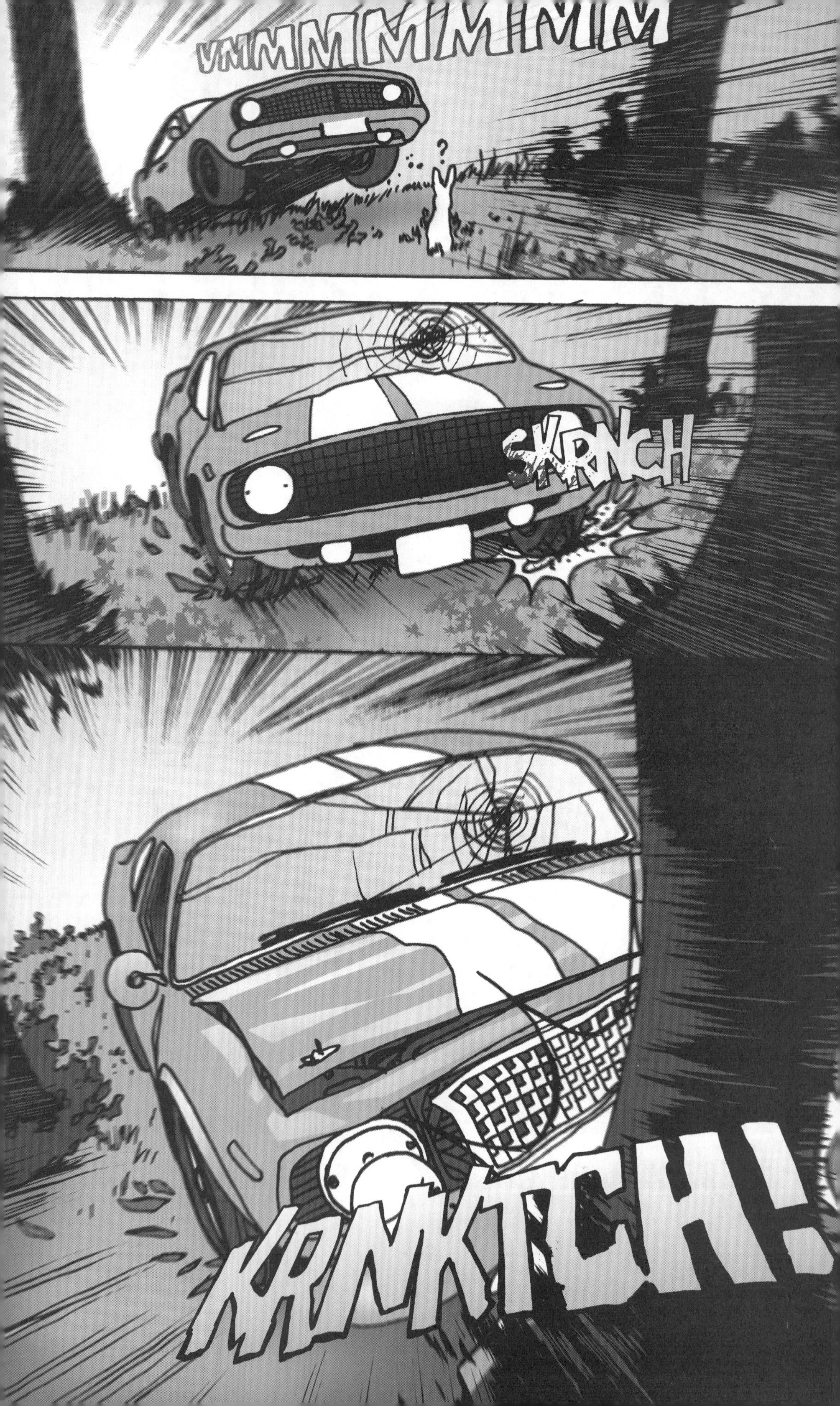

VMMMMMMMMM
?
SKRNCH
KRNKTCH!

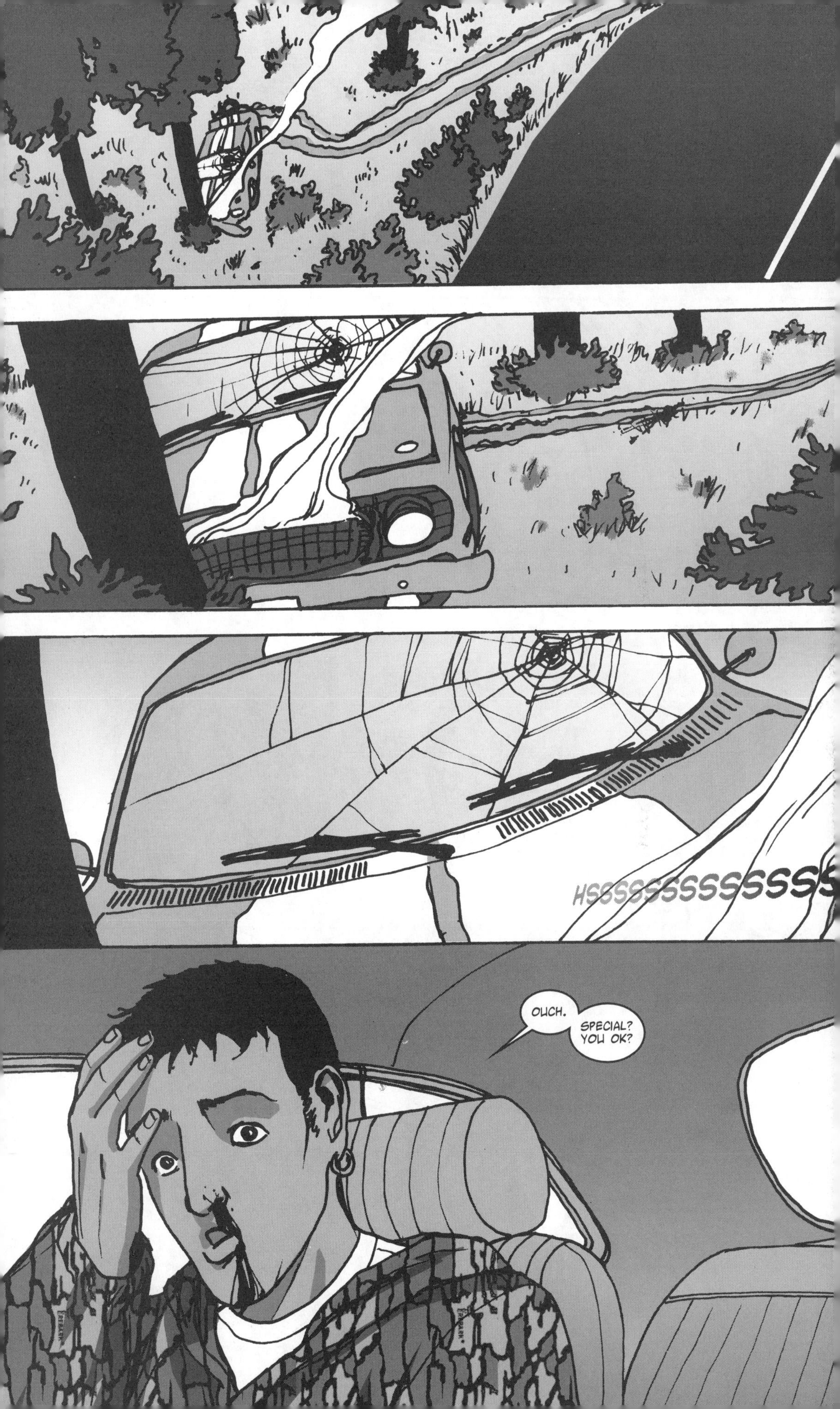
HSSSSSSSSSSSSSS
OUCH.
SPECIAL? YOU OK?

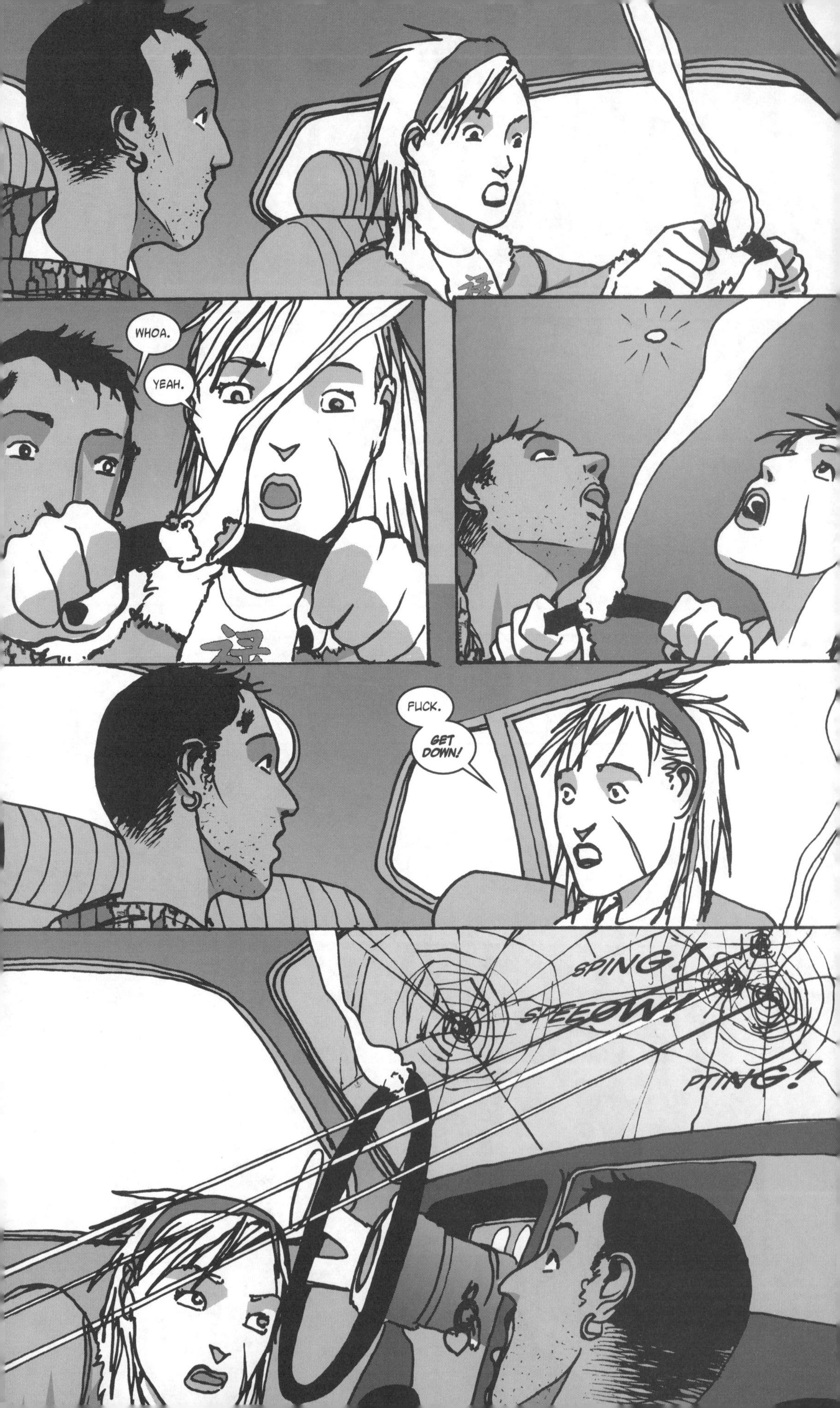
WHOA.
YEAH.
FUCK.
GET DOWN!
SPING!
SPEEOW!
PTING!

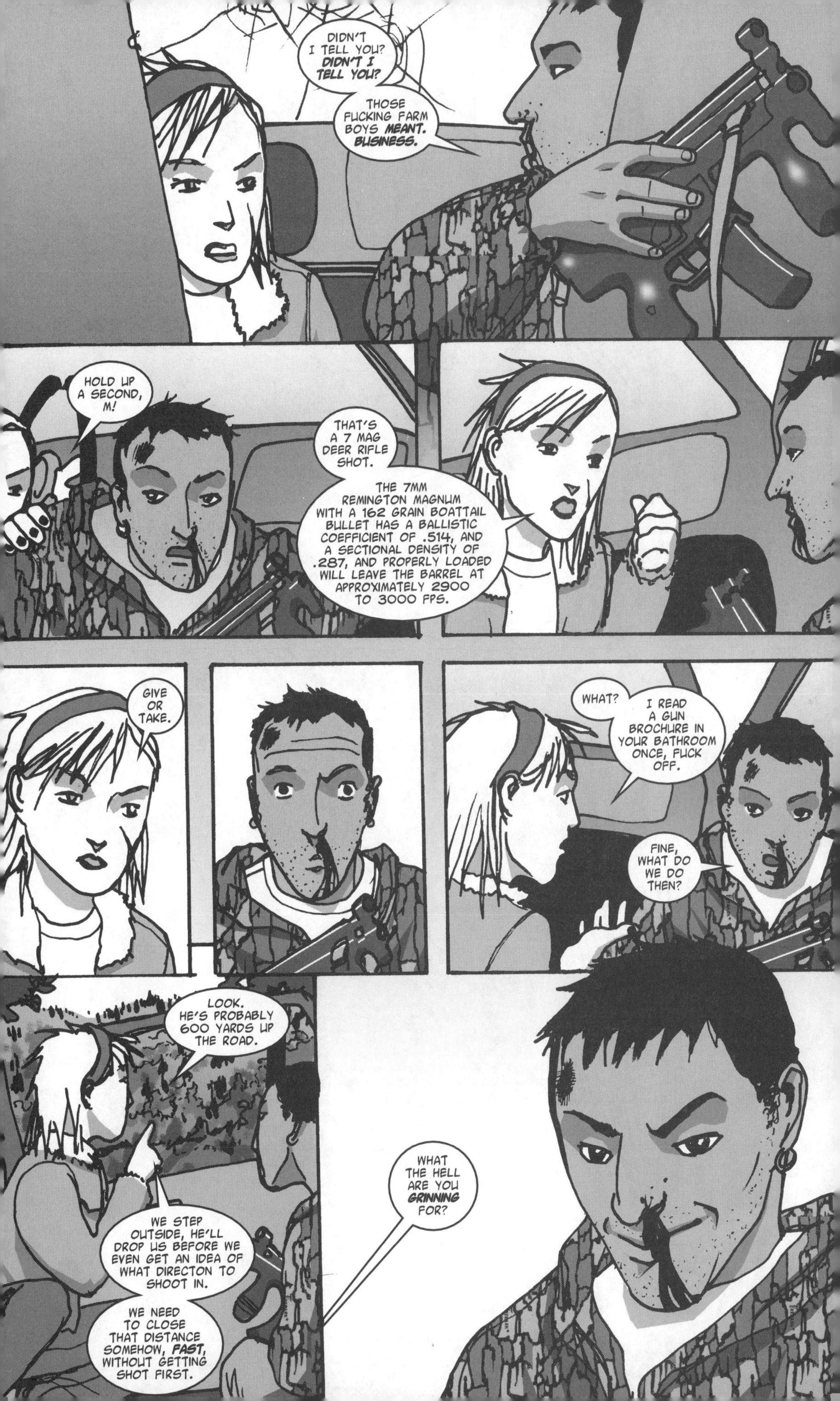
DIDN'T I TELL YOU? **DIDN'T I TELL YOU?**
THOSE FUCKING FARM BOYS **MEANT. BUSINESS.**
HOLD UP A SECOND, M!
THAT'S A 7 MAG DEER RIFLE SHOT.
THE 7MM REMINGTON MAGNUM WITH A 162 GRAIN BOATTAIL BULLET HAS A BALLISTIC COEFFICIENT OF .514, AND A SECTIONAL DENSITY OF .287, AND PROPERLY LOADED WILL LEAVE THE BARREL AT APPROXIMATELY 2900 TO 3000 FPS.
GIVE OR TAKE.
WHAT?
I READ A GUN BROCHURE IN YOUR BATHROOM ONCE, FUCK OFF.
FINE, WHAT DO WE DO THEN?
LOOK. HE'S PROBABLY 600 YARDS UP THE ROAD.
WE STEP OUTSIDE, HE'LL DROP US BEFORE WE EVEN GET AN IDEA OF WHAT DIRECTON TO SHOOT IN.
WE NEED TO CLOSE THAT DISTANCE SOMEHOW, **FAST**, WITHOUT GETTING SHOT FIRST.
WHAT THE HELL ARE YOU **GRINNING** FOR?

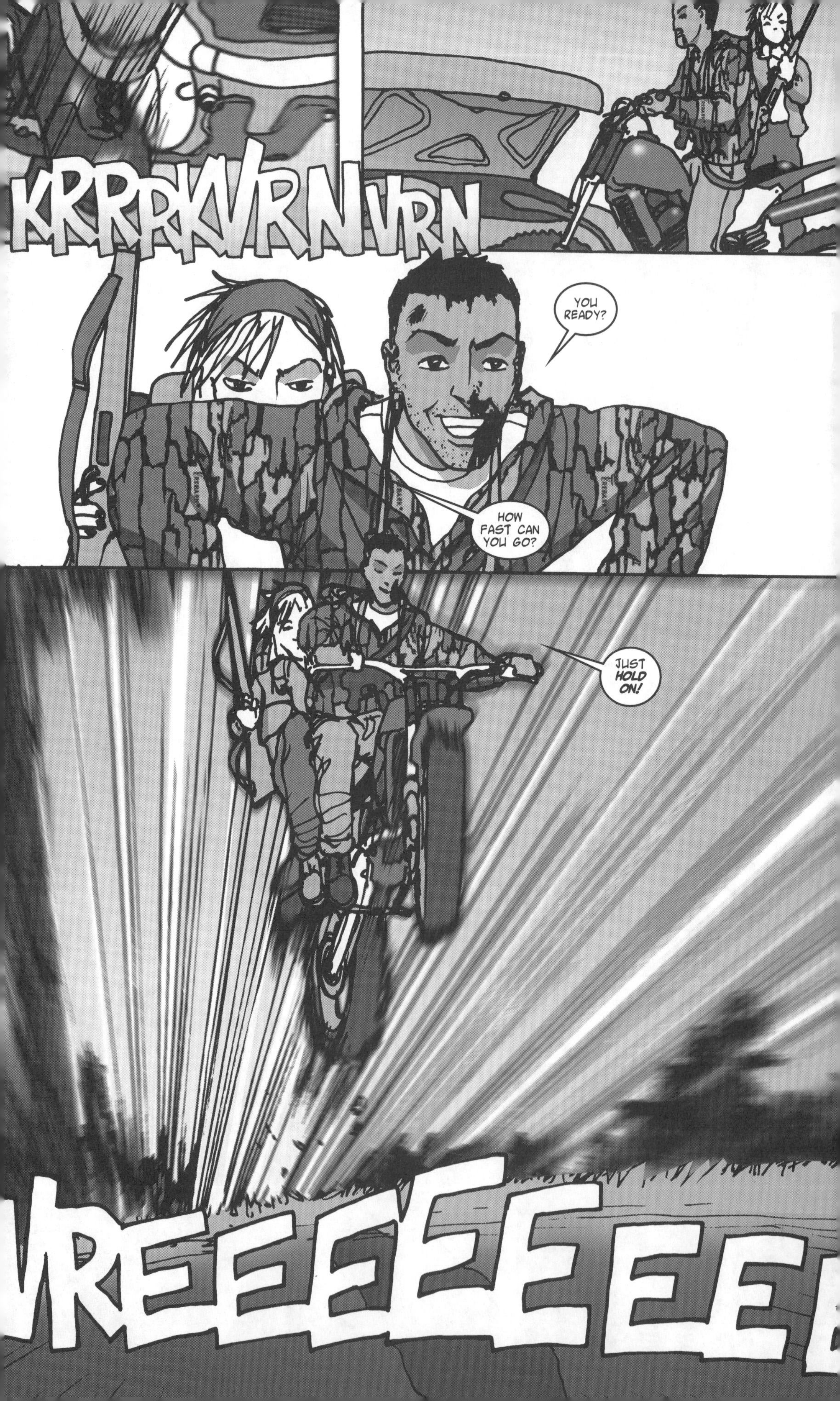
KRRRKVRN VRN
YOU READY?
HOW FAST CAN YOU GO?
JUST HOLD ON!
VREEEEEEEE

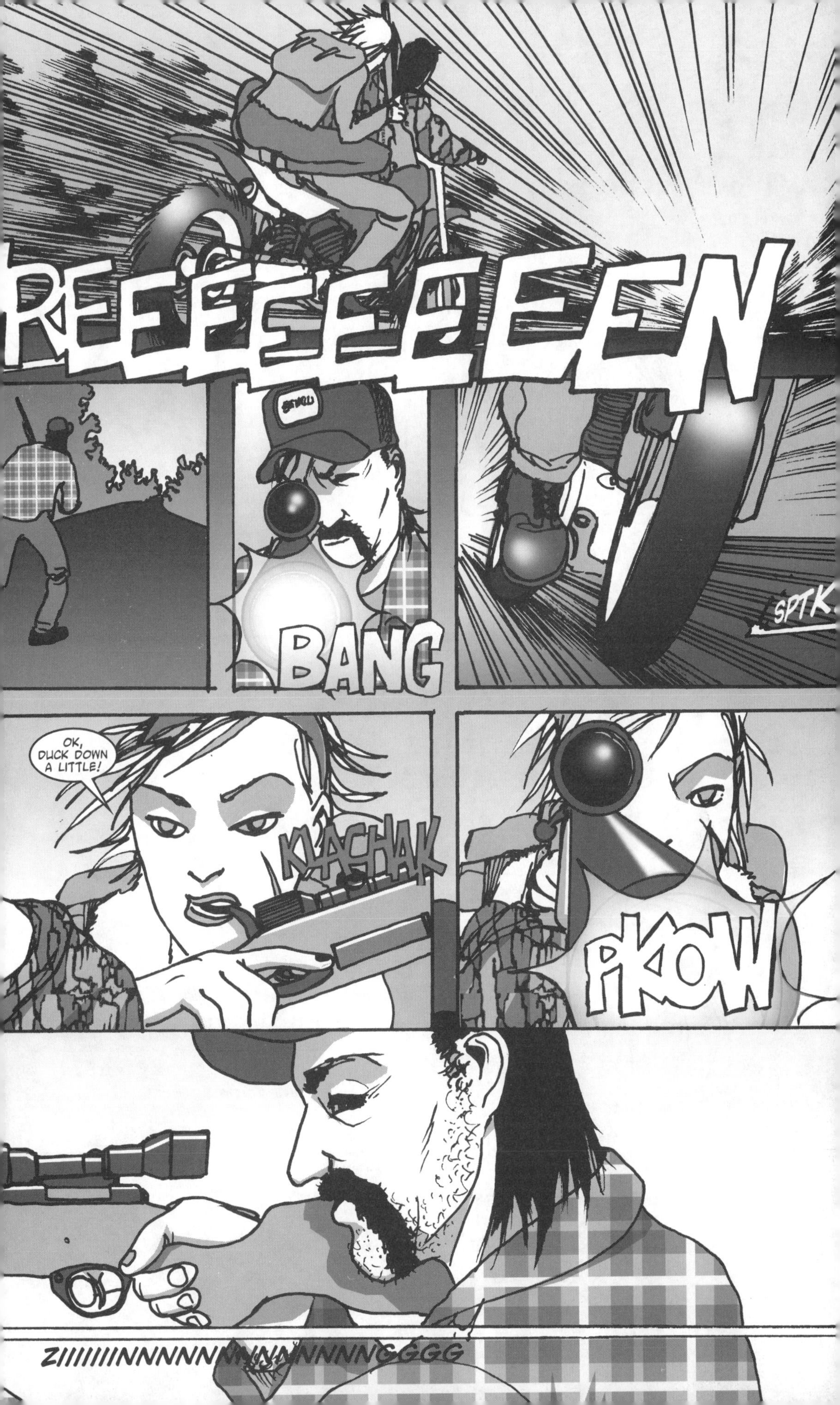
REEEEEEEEN
BANG
SPTK
OK, DUCK DOWN A LITTLE!
KLACHAK
PKOW
ZIIIIIINNNNNNNNNNNNNNNGGGG

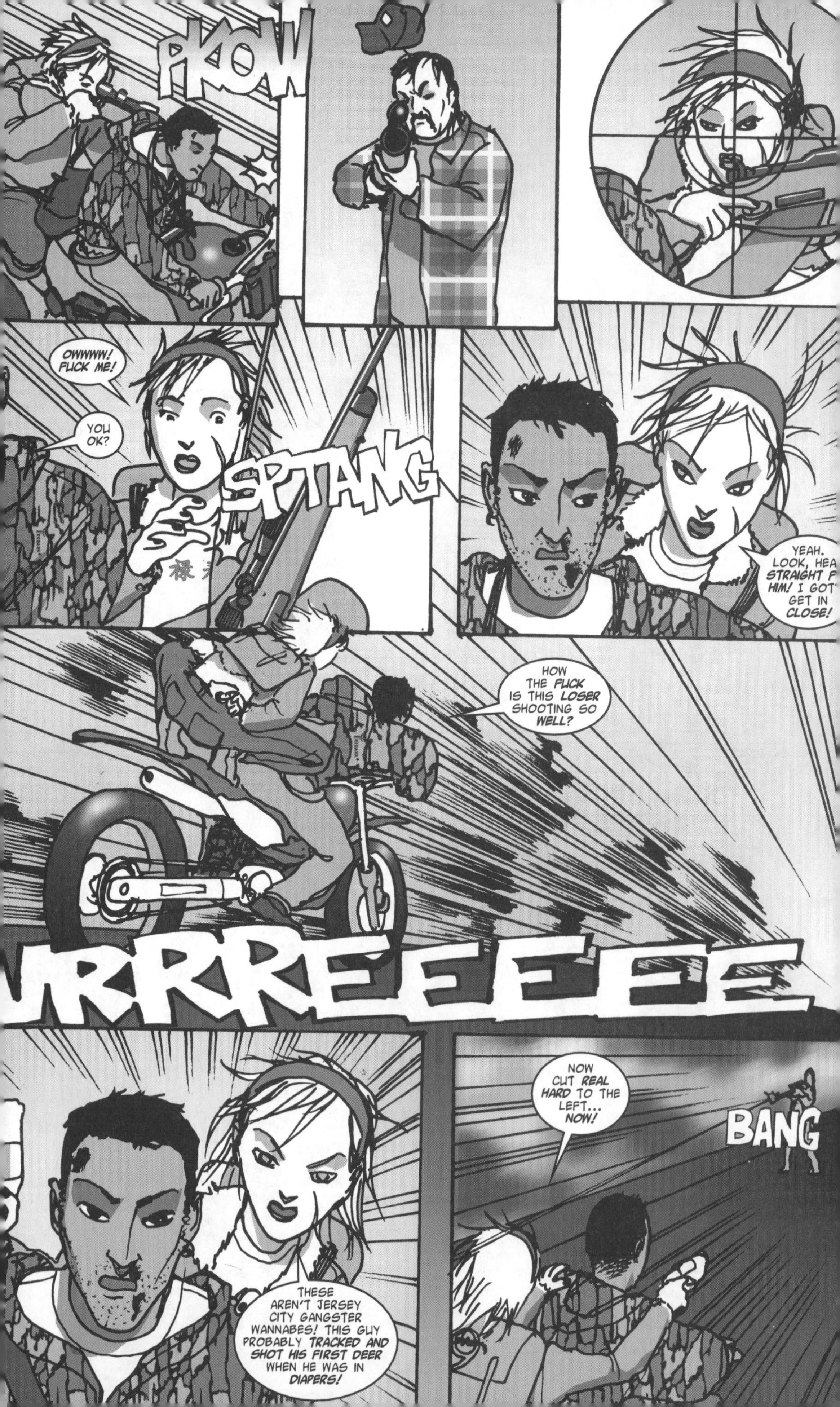
PKOW
OWWWW! FUCK ME!
YOU OK?
SPTANG
YEAH. LOOK, HEA STRAIGHT F HIM! I GOT GET IN CLOSE!
HOW THE FUCK IS THIS LOSER SHOOTING SO WELL?
RRREEEEE
THESE AREN'T JERSEY CITY GANGSTER WANNABES! THIS GUY PROBABLY TRACKED AND SHOT HIS FIRST DEER WHEN HE WAS IN DIAPERS!
NOW CUT REAL HARD TO THE LEFT... NOW!
BANG

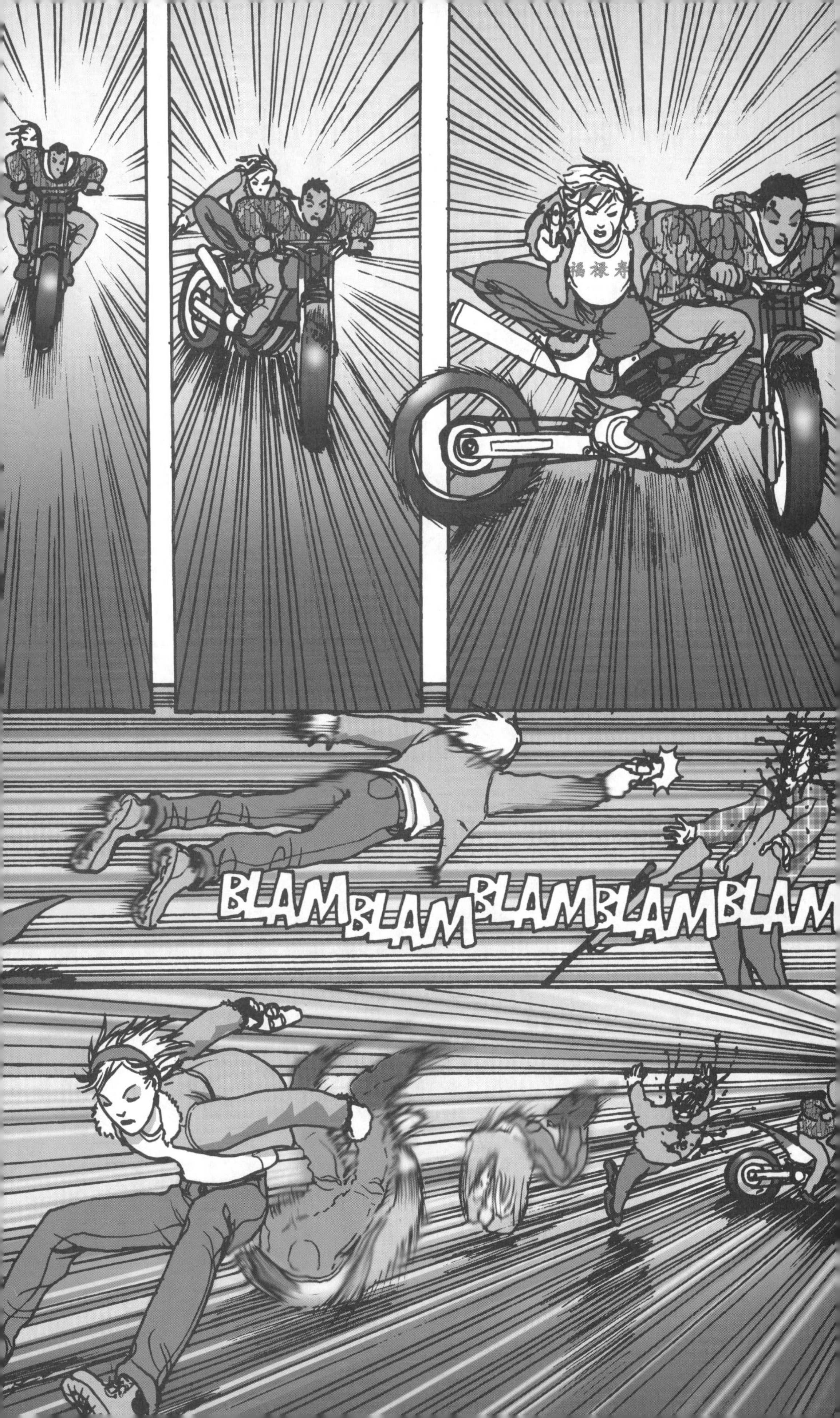

福禄寿
BLAM BLAM BLAM BLAM BLAM

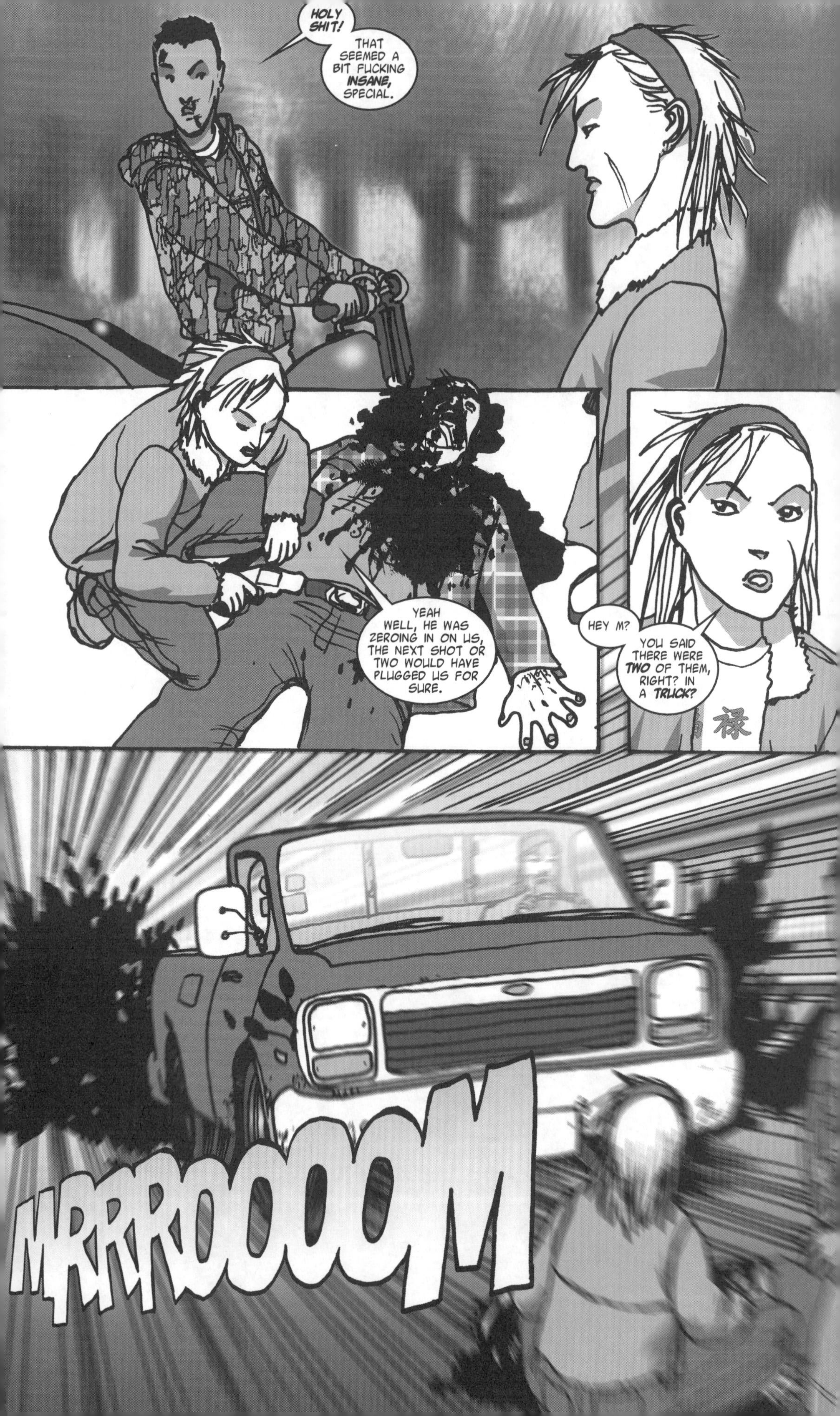
HOLY SHIT!
THAT SEEMED A BIT FUCKING INSANE, SPECIAL.
YEAH WELL, HE WAS ZEROING IN ON US, THE NEXT SHOT OR TWO WOULD HAVE PLUGGED US FOR SURE.
HEY M?
YOU SAID THERE WERE TWO OF THEM, RIGHT? IN A TRUCK?
MRRROOOOM

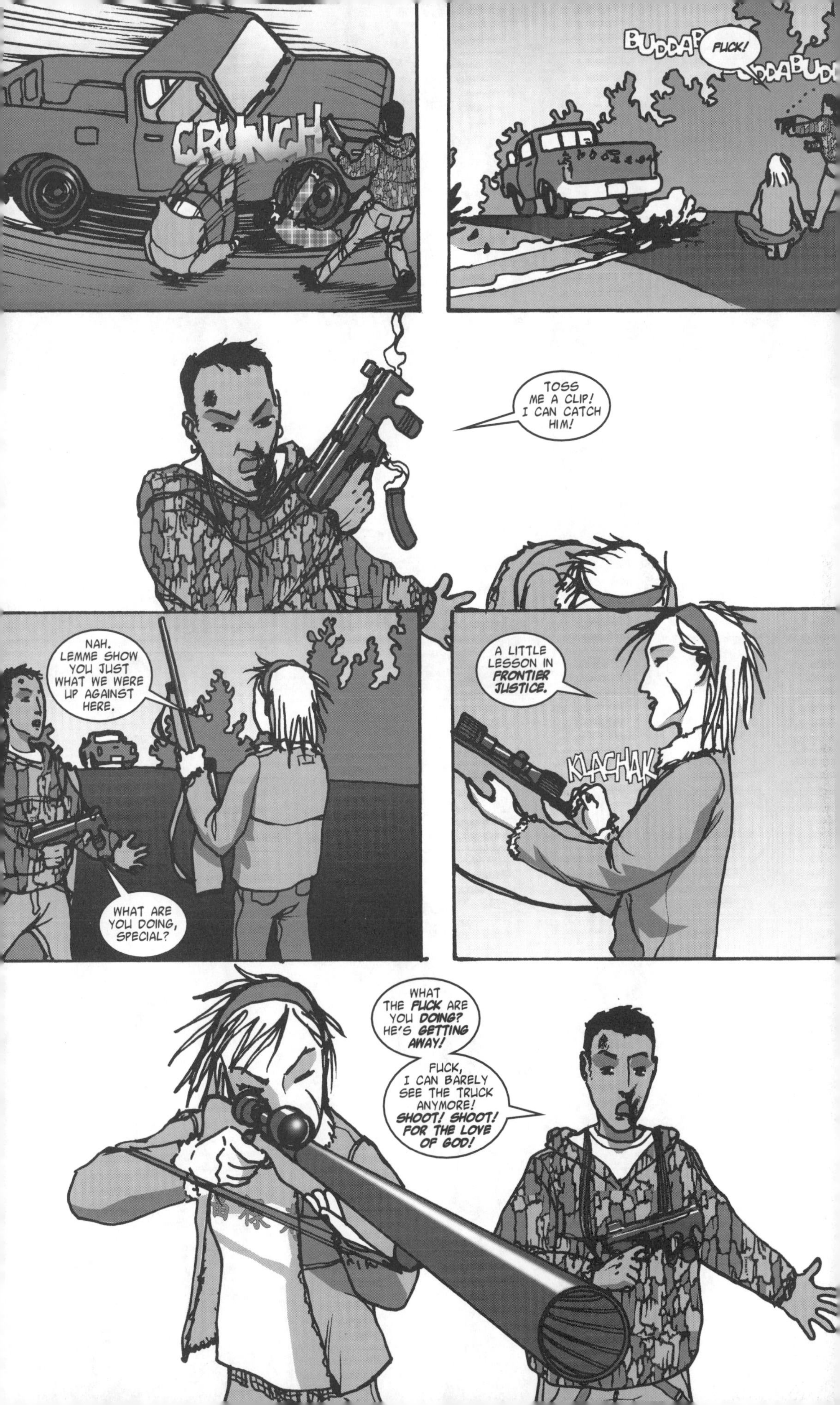
CRUNCH
BUDDAP
FUCK!
DDABUD
TOSS ME A CLIP! I CAN CATCH HIM!
NAH. LEMME SHOW YOU JUST WHAT WE WERE UP AGAINST HERE.
WHAT ARE YOU DOING, SPECIAL?
A LITTLE LESSON IN FRONTIER JUSTICE.
KLACHAK
WHAT THE FUCK ARE YOU DOING? HE'S GETTING AWAY!
FUCK, I CAN BARELY SEE THE TRUCK ANYMORE! SHOOT! SHOOT! FOR THE LOVE OF GOD!

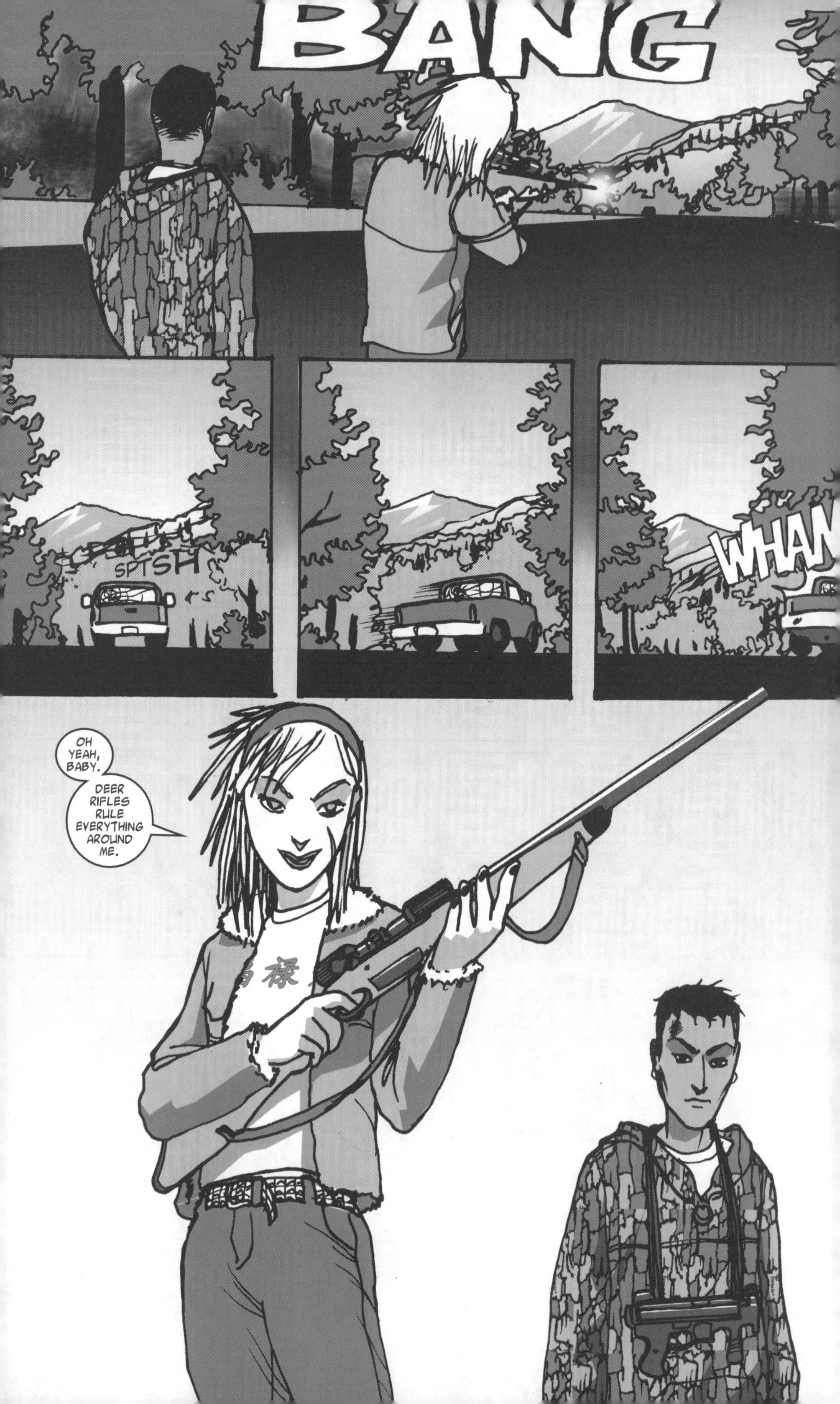
BANG
SPTSH
WHAM
OH YEAH, BABY.
DEER RIFLES RULE EVERYTHING AROUND ME.

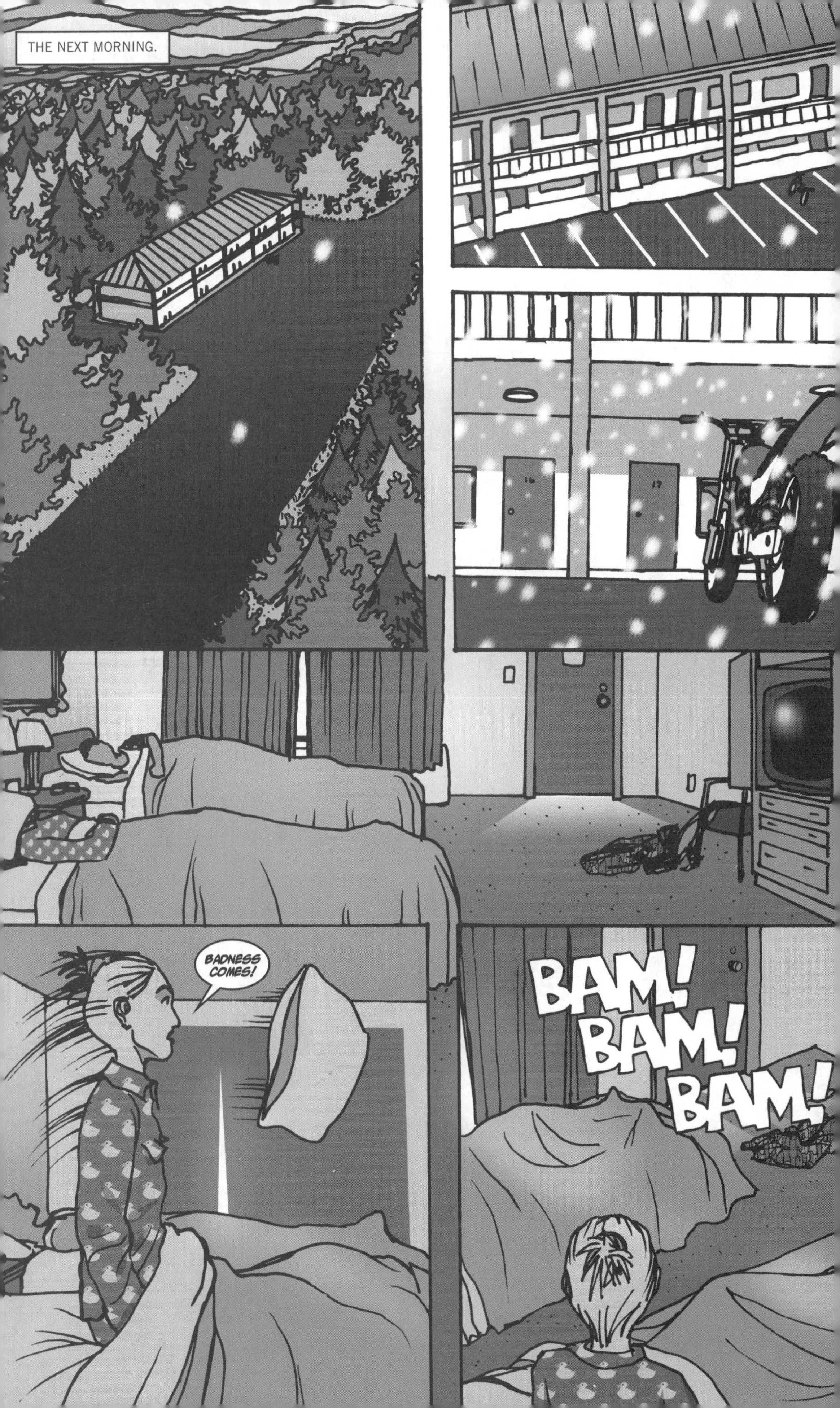

THE NEXT MORNING.
16
17
BADNESS COMES!
BAM! BAM! BAM!

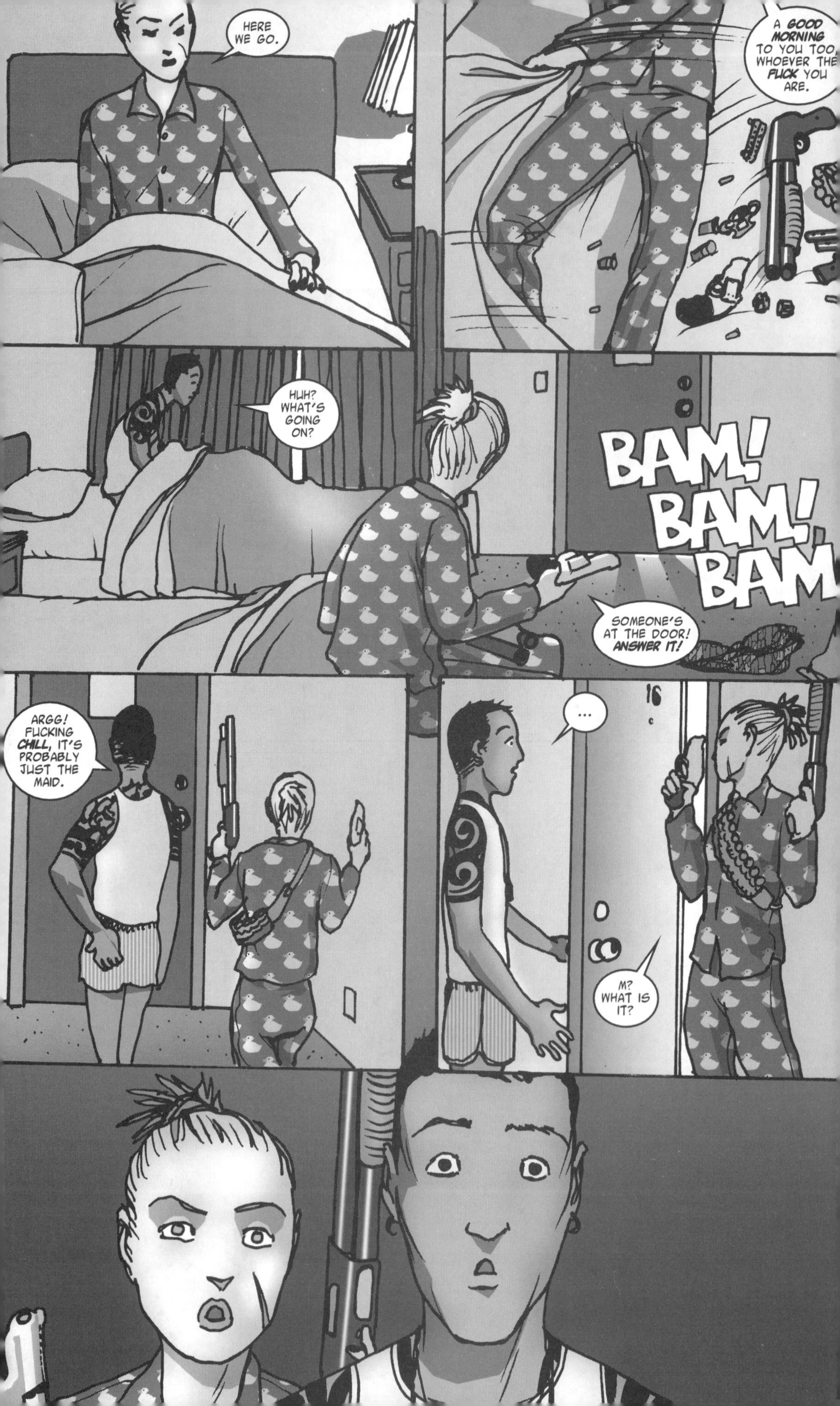
HERE WE GO.
A GOOD MORNING TO YOU TOO, WHOEVER THE FUCK YOU ARE.
HUH? WHAT'S GOING ON?
BAM! BAM! BAM
SOMEONE'S AT THE DOOR! ANSWER IT!
ARGG! FUCKING CHILL, IT'S PROBABLY JUST THE MAID.
...
M? WHAT IS IT?

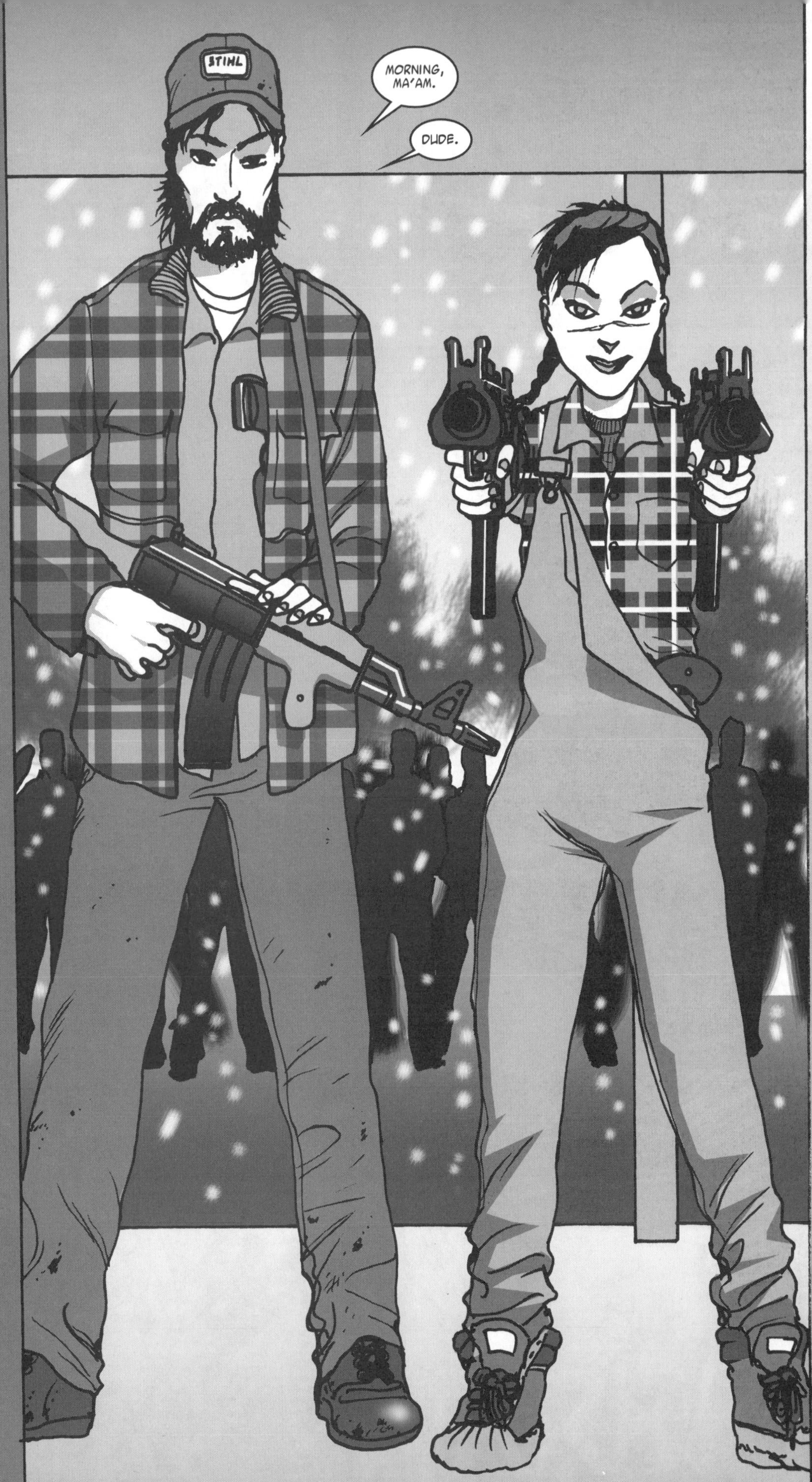
MORNING, MA'AM.
DUDE.

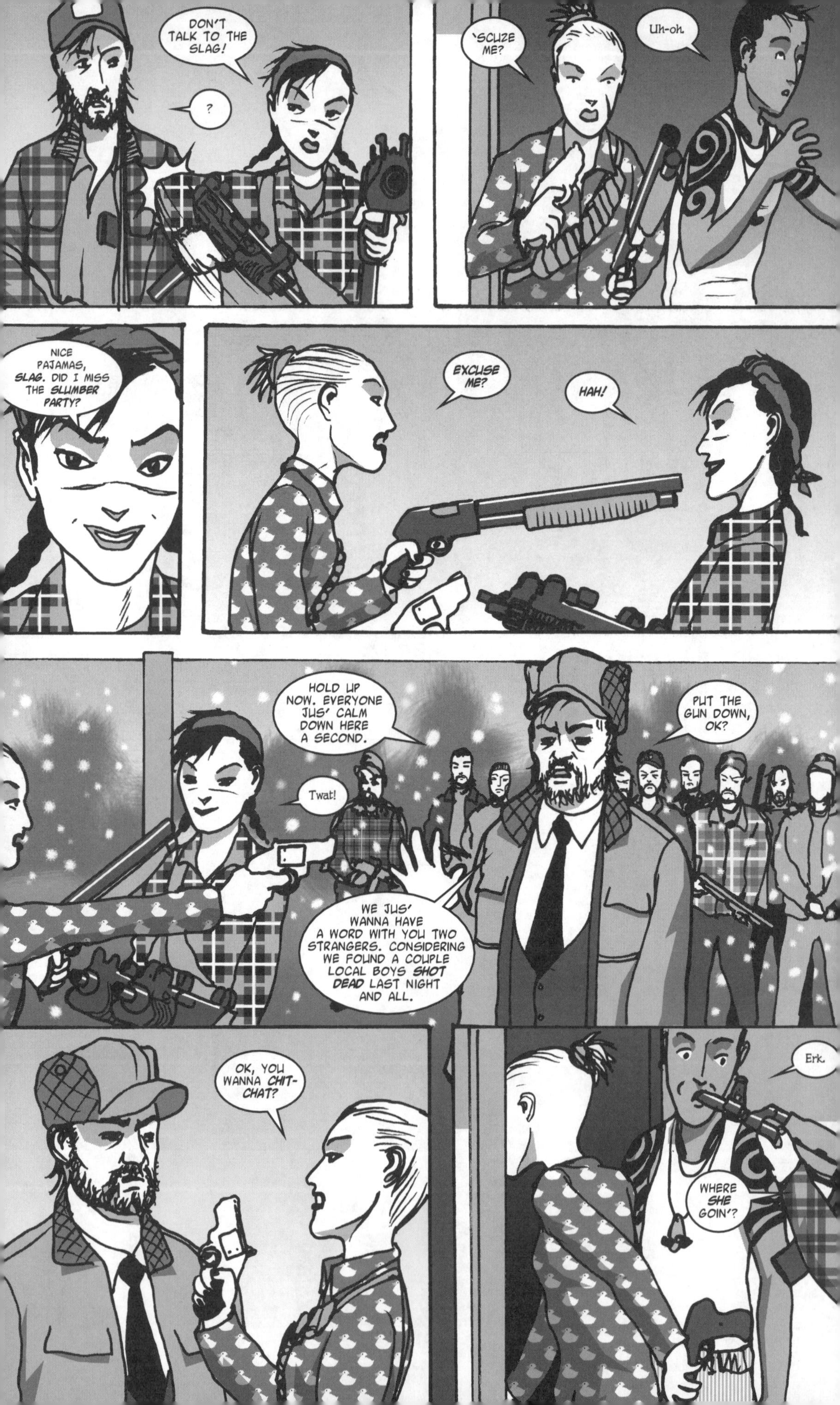
DON'T TALK TO THE SLAG!
?
'SCUZE ME?
Uh-oh.
NICE PAJAMAS, SLAG. DID I MISS THE SLUMBER PARTY?
EXCUSE ME?
HAH!
HOLD UP NOW. EVERYONE JUS' CALM DOWN HERE A SECOND.
Twat!
PUT THE GUN DOWN, OK?
WE JUS' WANNA HAVE A WORD WITH YOU TWO STRANGERS. CONSIDERING WE FOUND A COUPLE LOCAL BOYS SHOT DEAD LAST NIGHT AND ALL.
OK, YOU WANNA CHIT-CHAT?
Erk.
WHERE SHE GOIN'?

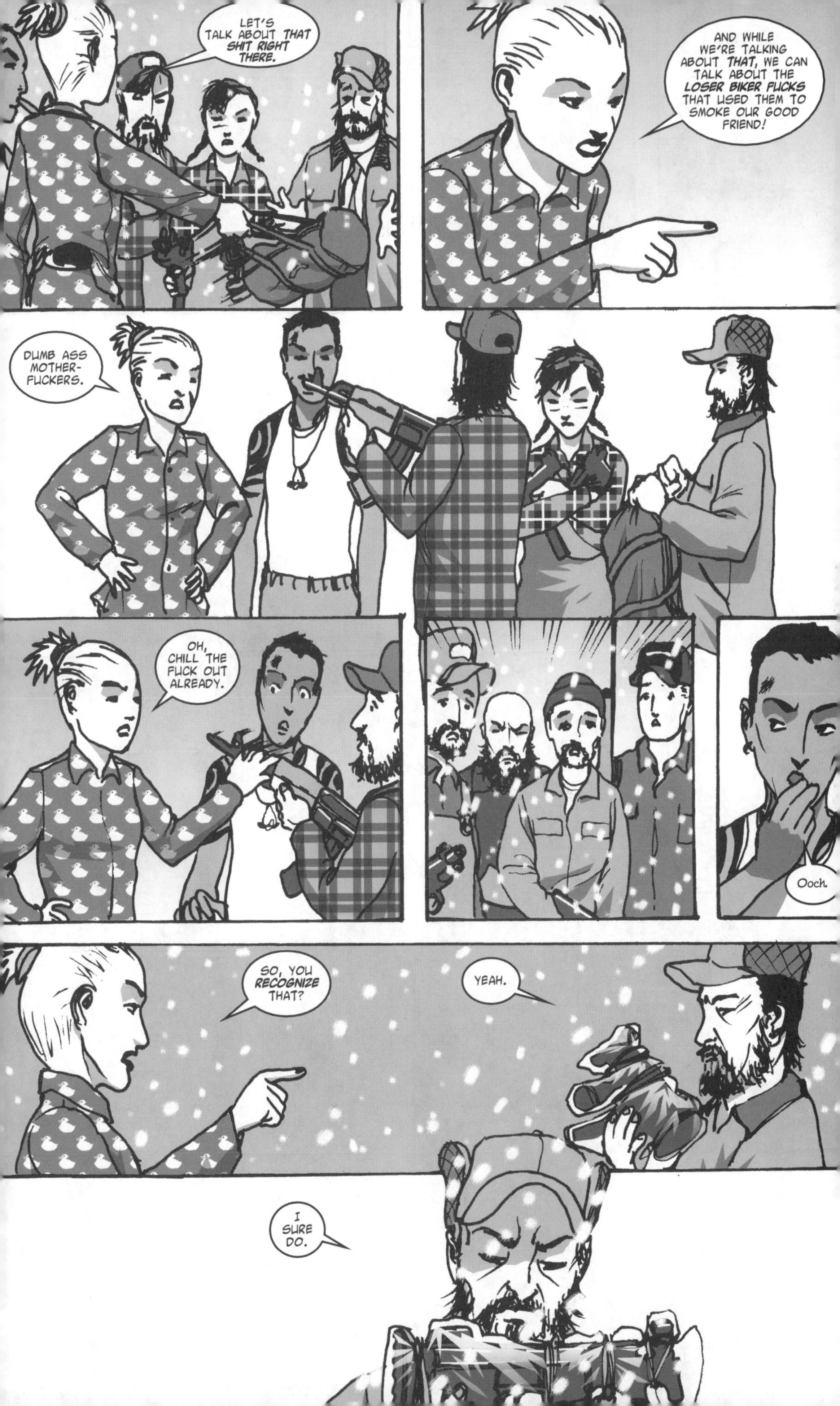
LET'S TALK ABOUT THAT SHIT RIGHT THERE.
AND WHILE WE'RE TALKING ABOUT THAT, WE CAN TALK ABOUT THE LOSER BIKER FUCKS THAT USED THEM TO SMOKE OUR GOOD FRIEND!
DUMB ASS MOTHER-FUCKERS.
OH, CHILL THE FUCK OUT ALREADY.
Ooch.
SO, YOU RECOGNIZE THAT?
YEAH.
I SURE DO.

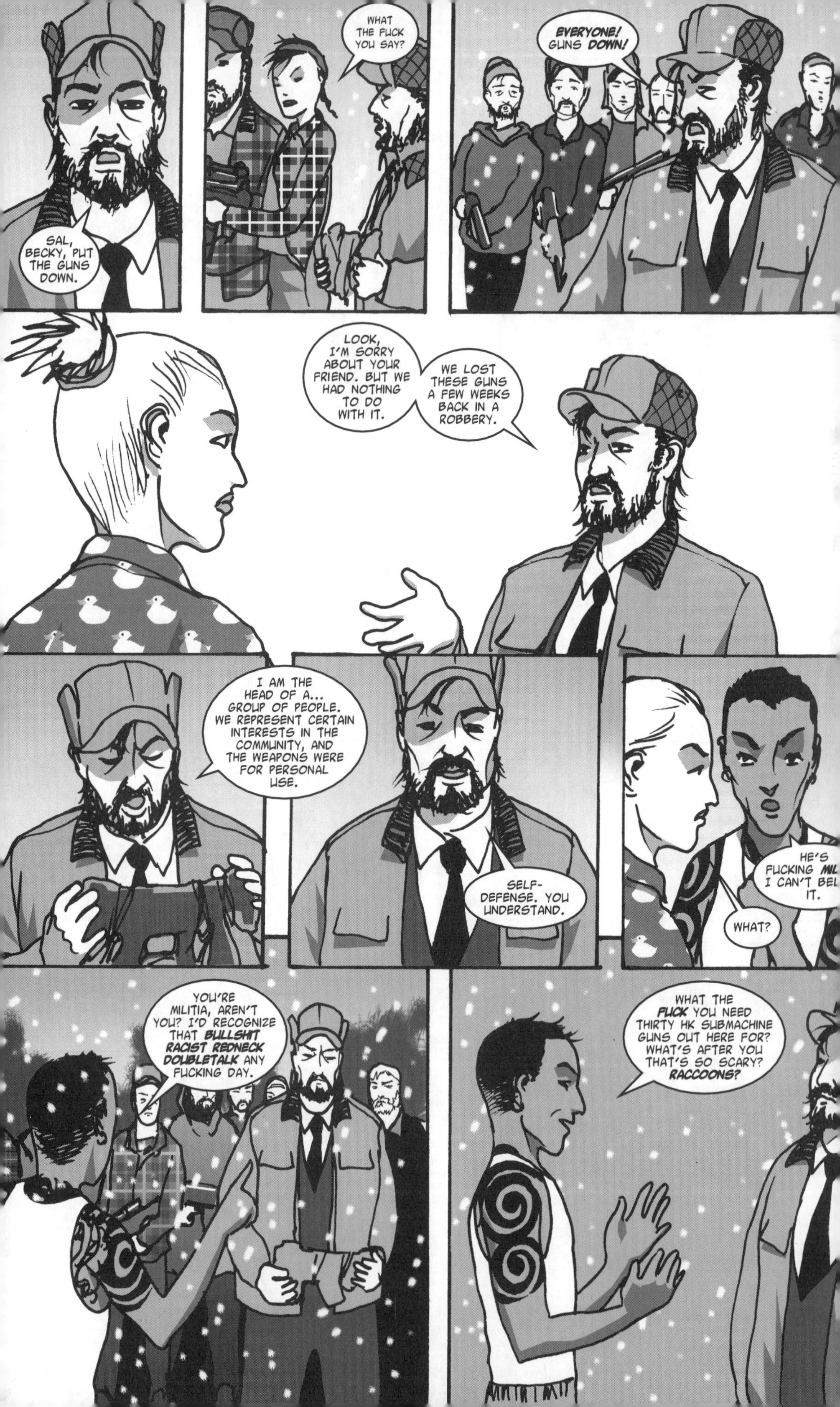
SAL, BECKY, PUT THE GUNS DOWN.
WHAT THE FUCK YOU SAY?
EVERYONE! GUNS DOWN!
LOOK, I'M SORRY ABOUT YOUR FRIEND. BUT WE HAD NOTHING TO DO WITH IT.
WE LOST THESE GUNS A FEW WEEKS BACK IN A ROBBERY.
I AM THE HEAD OF A... GROUP OF PEOPLE. WE REPRESENT CERTAIN INTERESTS IN THE COMMUNITY, AND THE WEAPONS WERE FOR PERSONAL USE.
SELF-DEFENSE. YOU UNDERSTAND.
WHAT?
YOU'RE MILITIA, AREN'T YOU? I'D RECOGNIZE THAT BULLSHIT RACIST REDNECK DOUBLETALK ANY FUCKING DAY.
WHAT THE FUCK YOU NEED THIRTY HK SUBMACHINE GUNS OUT HERE FOR? WHAT'S AFTER YOU THAT'S SO SCARY? RACCOONS?

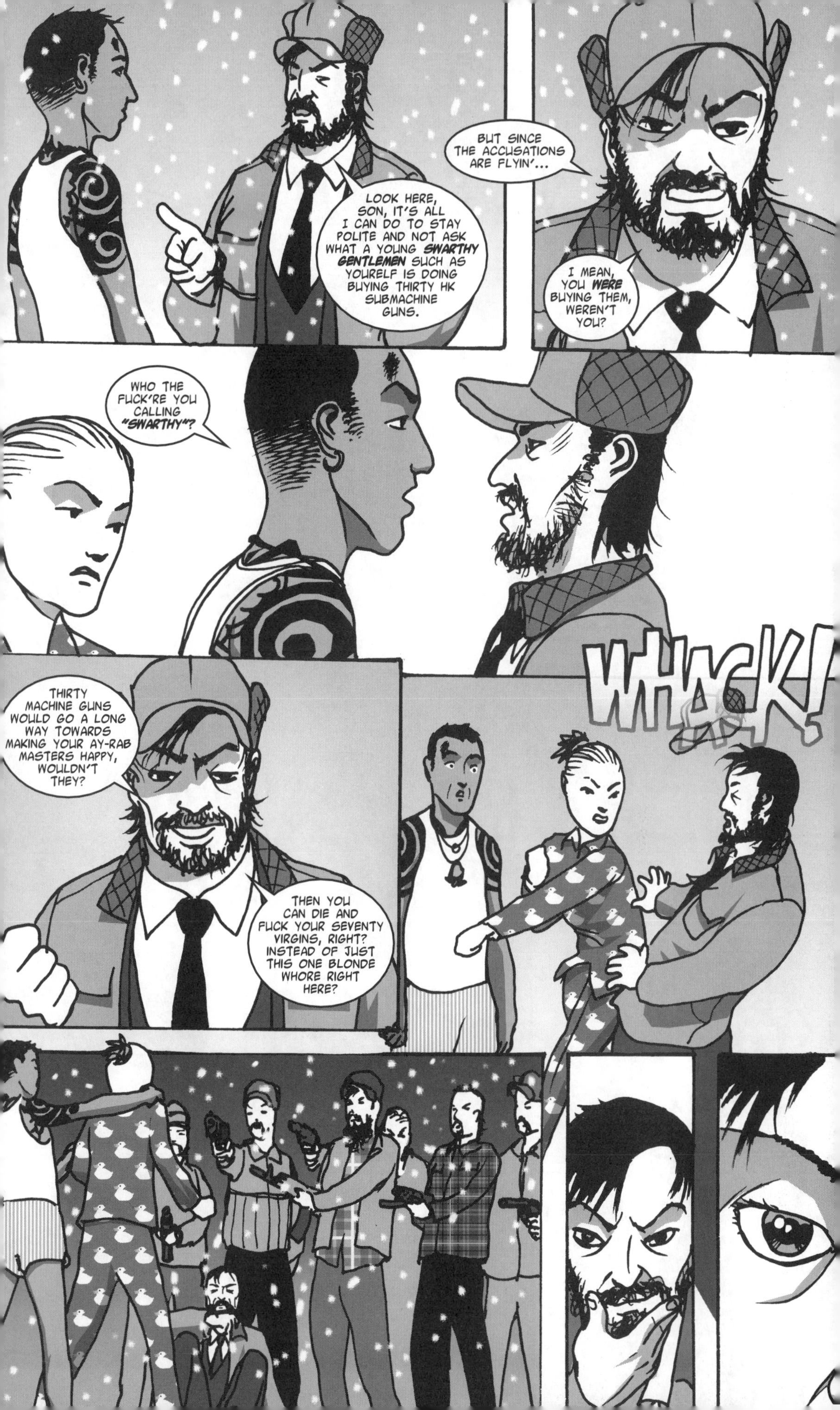

LOOK HERE, SON, IT'S ALL I CAN DO TO STAY POLITE AND NOT ASK WHAT A YOUNG SWARTHY GENTLEMEN SUCH AS YOURELF IS DOING BUYING THIRTY HK SUBMACHINE GUNS.
BUT SINCE THE ACCUSATIONS ARE FLYIN'...
I MEAN, YOU WERE BUYING THEM, WEREN'T YOU?
WHO THE FUCK'RE YOU CALLING "SWARTHY"?
THIRTY MACHINE GUNS WOULD GO A LONG WAY TOWARDS MAKING YOUR AY-RAB MASTERS HAPPY, WOULDN'T THEY?
THEN YOU CAN DIE AND FUCK YOUR SEVENTY VIRGINS, RIGHT? INSTEAD OF JUST THIS ONE BLONDE WHORE RIGHT HERE?
WHACK!

OW!

OW!

...AND STAY OUT!

FUCKING LOSERS!

HE SAID WE COULD *SHOOT YA*, BUT IT WAS MORE FUN TO CLOBBER YOU AND STEAL ALL YOUR GUNS!

I'VE HEARD OF YOU TWO, YOU KNOW. WORD TRAVELS FAR IN OUR LINE OF BUSINESS. WE DO HAVE RESPECT FOR THAT. THAT'S WHY WE DIDN'T WASTE YA.

I JUST WANT YOU TO KNOW THERE'S NO HARD FEELINGS. YER TRYIN' TO MAKE THE TALL DOLLARS JUST LIKE WE ARE.

Cunts!

WE'RE NO MILITIA. FUCK THAT SHIT. BUT WE DO HATE DARKIES AND CITYFOLK JUST THE SAME. JUST SO YOU KNOW.

OH, AND *WE* RIPPED OFF AND SOLD THOSE GUNS TO THAT BIKER GANG. SORRY ABOUT YER BUT BUSINESS IS BUSINESS, YOU UNDERSTAND.

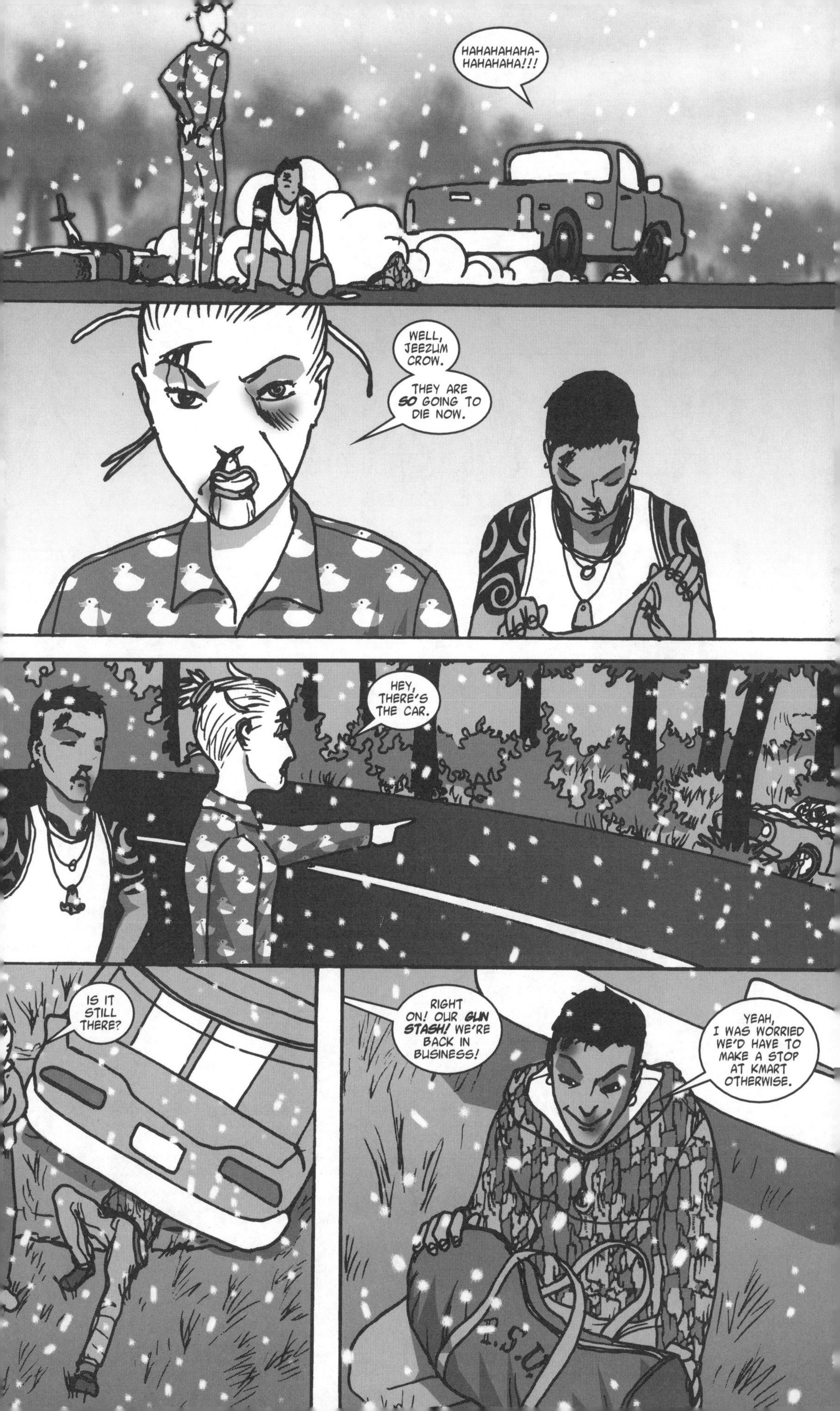
HAHAHAHAHA-HAHAHAHA!!!
WELL, JEEZUM CROW.
THEY ARE SO GOING TO DIE NOW.
HEY, THERE'S THE CAR.
IS IT STILL THERE?
RIGHT ON! OUR GUN STASH! WE'RE BACK IN BUSINESS!
YEAH, I WAS WORRIED WE'D HAVE TO MAKE A STOP AT KMART OTHERWISE.

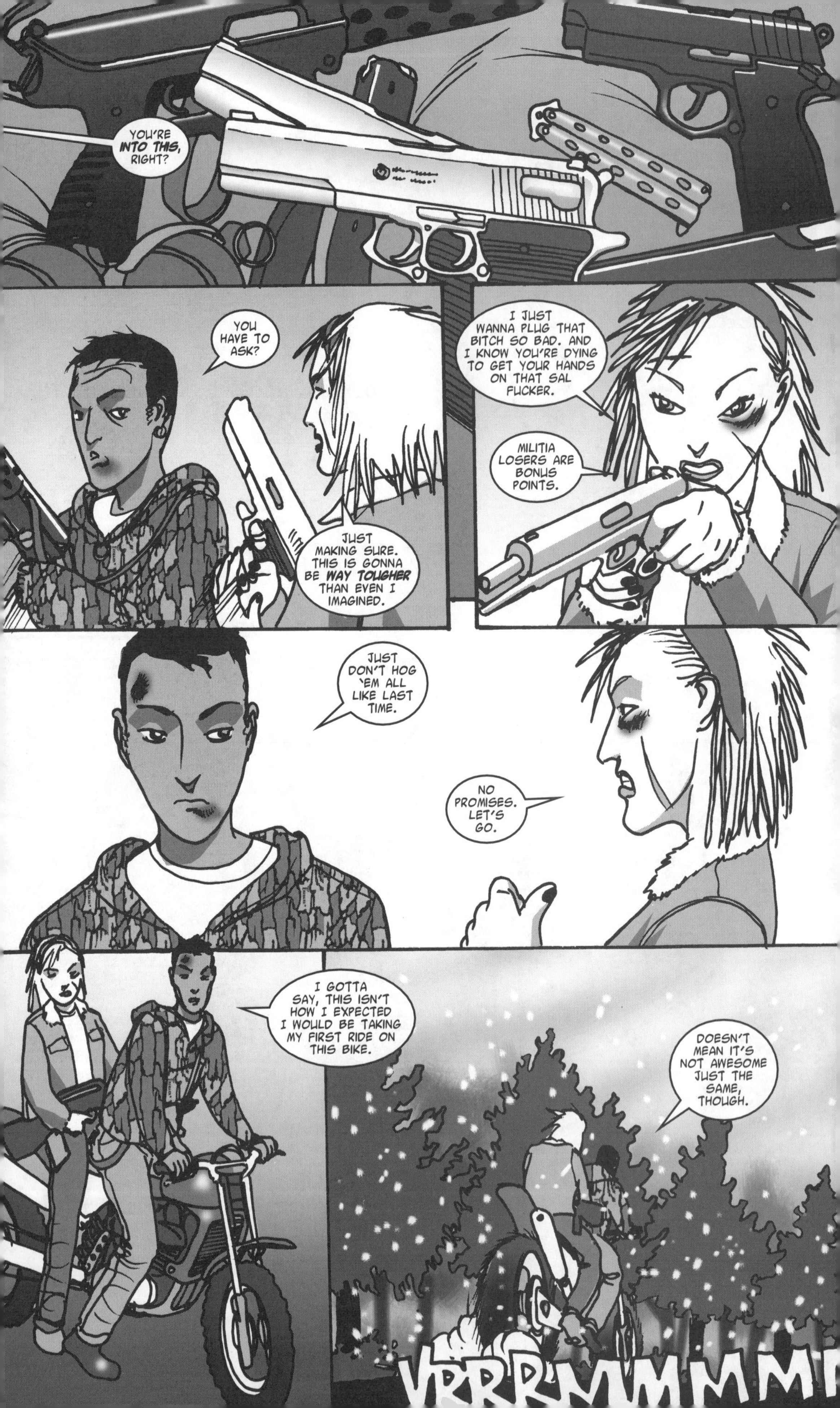

YOU'RE INTO THIS, RIGHT?
YOU HAVE TO ASK?
JUST MAKING SURE. THIS IS GONNA BE WAY TOUGHER THAN EVEN I IMAGINED.
I JUST WANNA PLUG THAT BITCH SO BAD. AND I KNOW YOU'RE DYING TO GET YOUR HANDS ON THAT SAL FUCKER.
MILITIA LOSERS ARE BONUS POINTS.
JUST DON'T HOG 'EM ALL LIKE LAST TIME.
NO PROMISES. LET'S GO.
I GOTTA SAY, THIS ISN'T HOW I EXPECTED I WOULD BE TAKING MY FIRST RIDE ON THIS BIKE.
DOESN'T MEAN IT'S NOT AWESOME JUST THE SAME, THOUGH.
VRRRMMMMMM

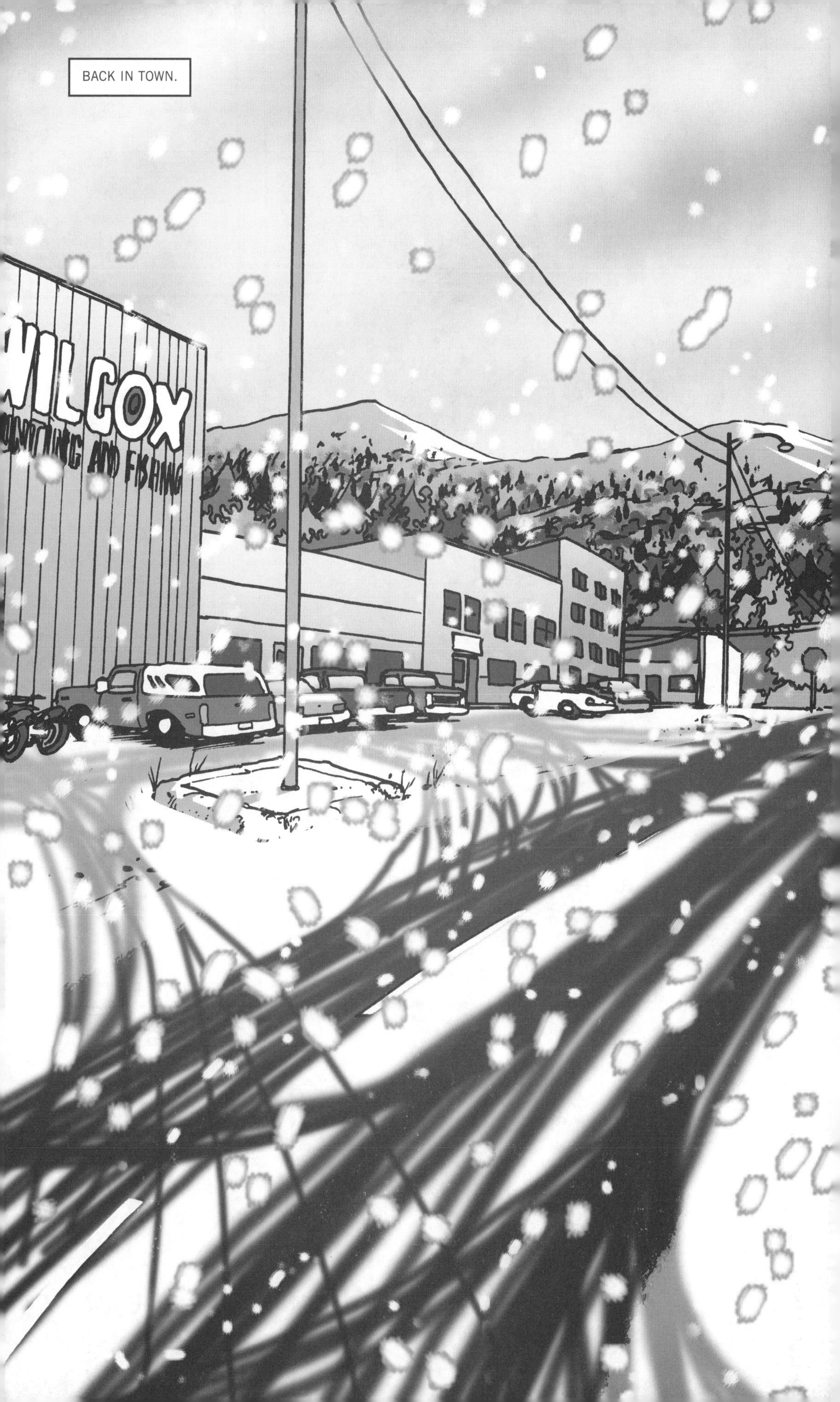
BACK IN TOWN.
WILCOX
AND FISHING

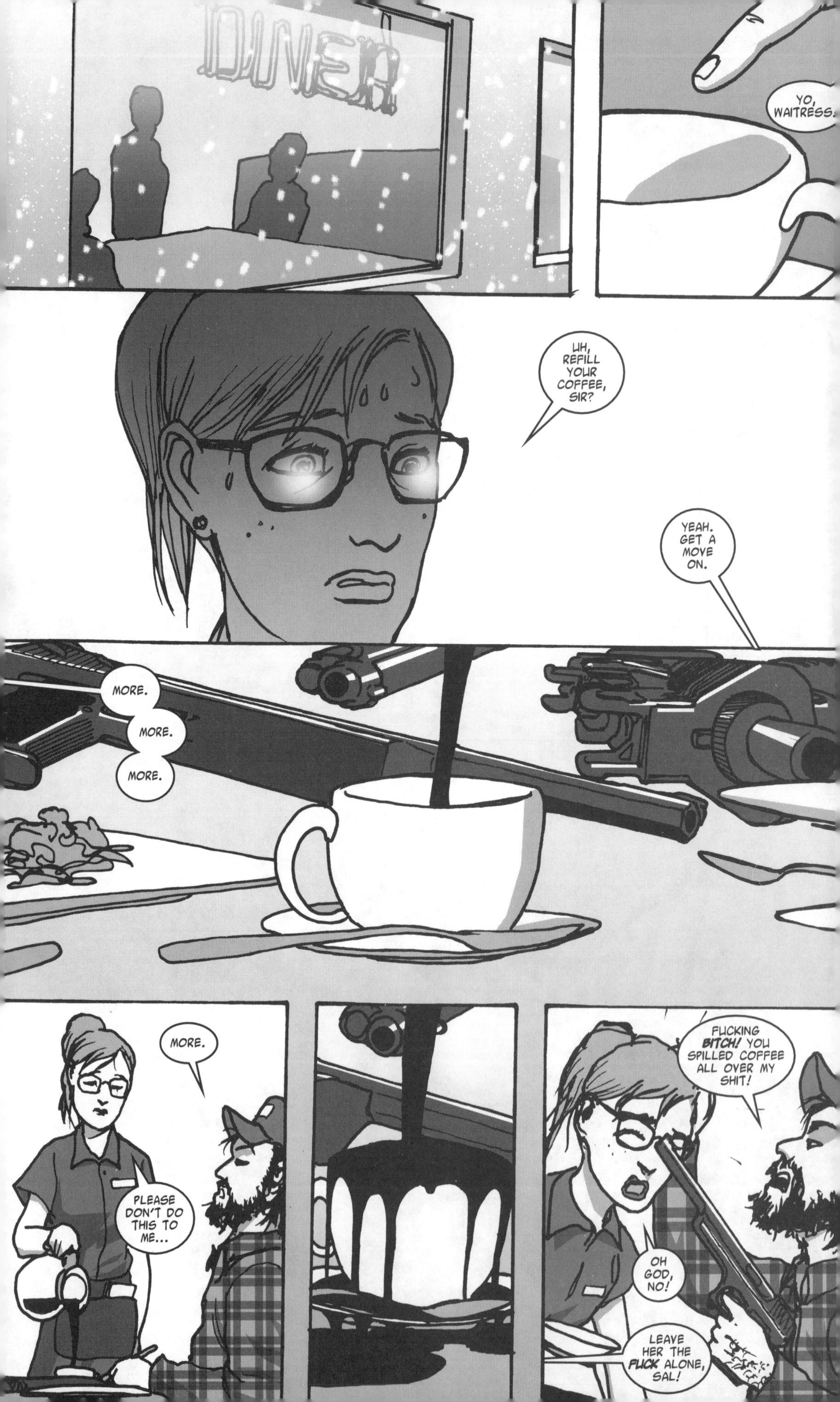
DINER
YO, WAITRESS.
UH, REFILL YOUR COFFEE, SIR?
YEAH. GET A MOVE ON.
MORE.
MORE.
MORE.
MORE.
PLEASE DON'T DO THIS TO ME...
FUCKING BITCH! YOU SPILLED COFFEE ALL OVER MY SHIT!
OH GOD, NO!
LEAVE HER THE FUCK ALONE, SAL!

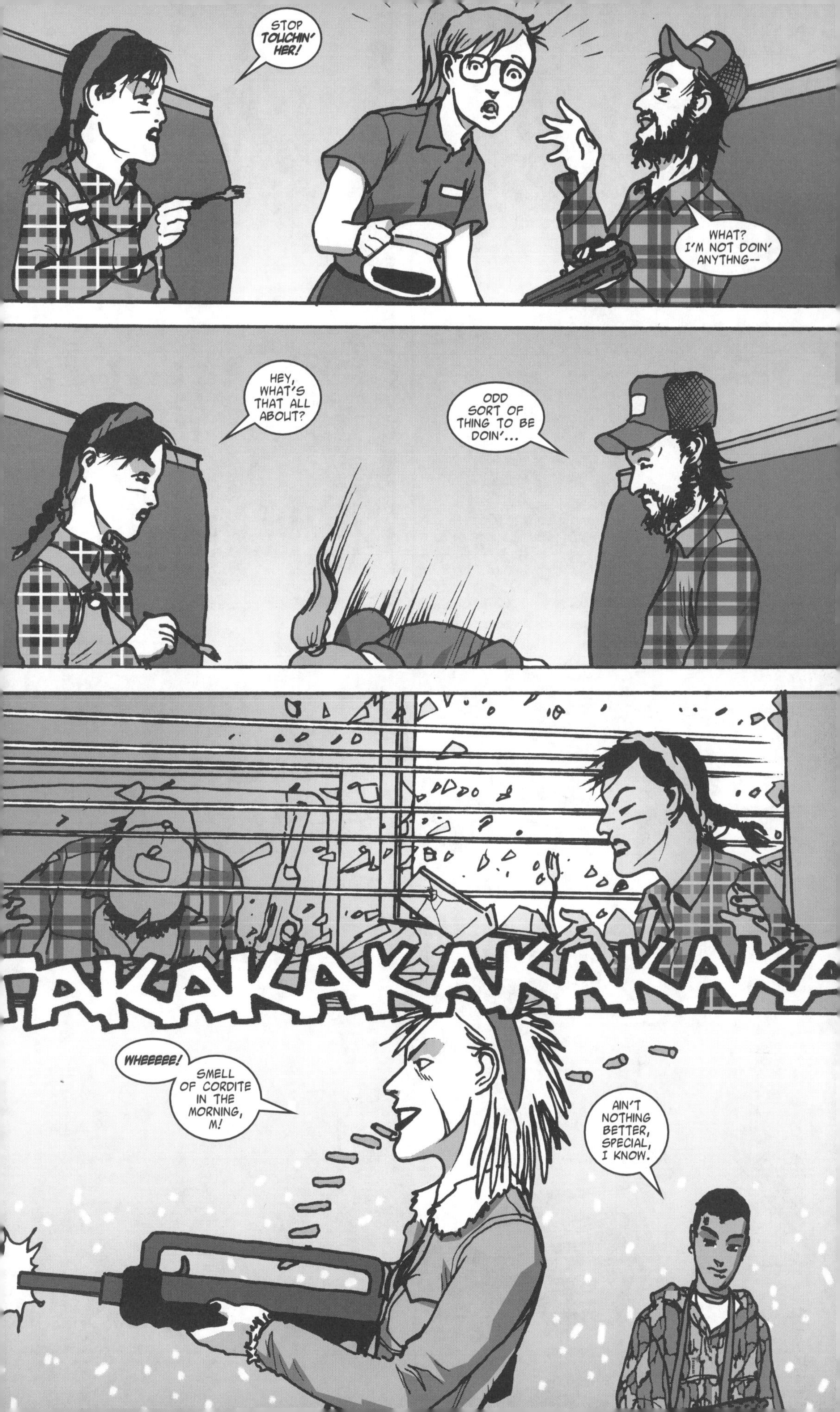
STOP TOUCHIN' HER!
WHAT? I'M NOT DOIN' ANYTHNG--
HEY, WHAT'S THAT ALL ABOUT?
ODD SORT OF THING TO BE DOIN'...
AKAKAKAKAKAKAKA
WHEEEEEE!
SMELL OF CORDITE IN THE MORNING, M!
AIN'T NOTHING BETTER, SPECIAL, I KNOW.

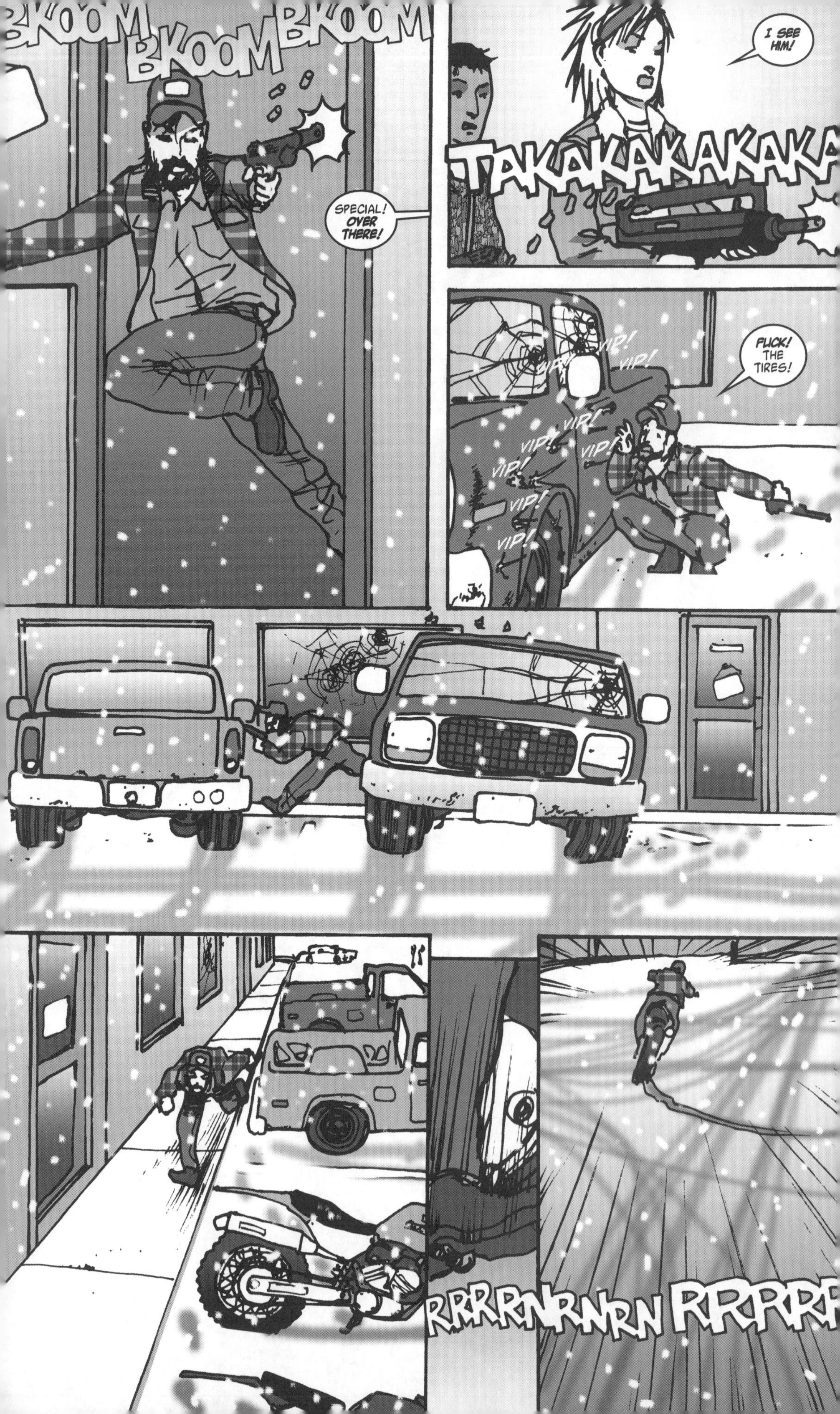
BKOOM BKOOM BKOOM
SPECIAL! OVER THERE!
I SEE HIM!
TAKAKAKAKAKAKA
VIP! VIP!
FUCK! THE TIRES!
VIP! VIP! VIP! VIP! VIP! VIP!
RRRRNRNRN RRRRR

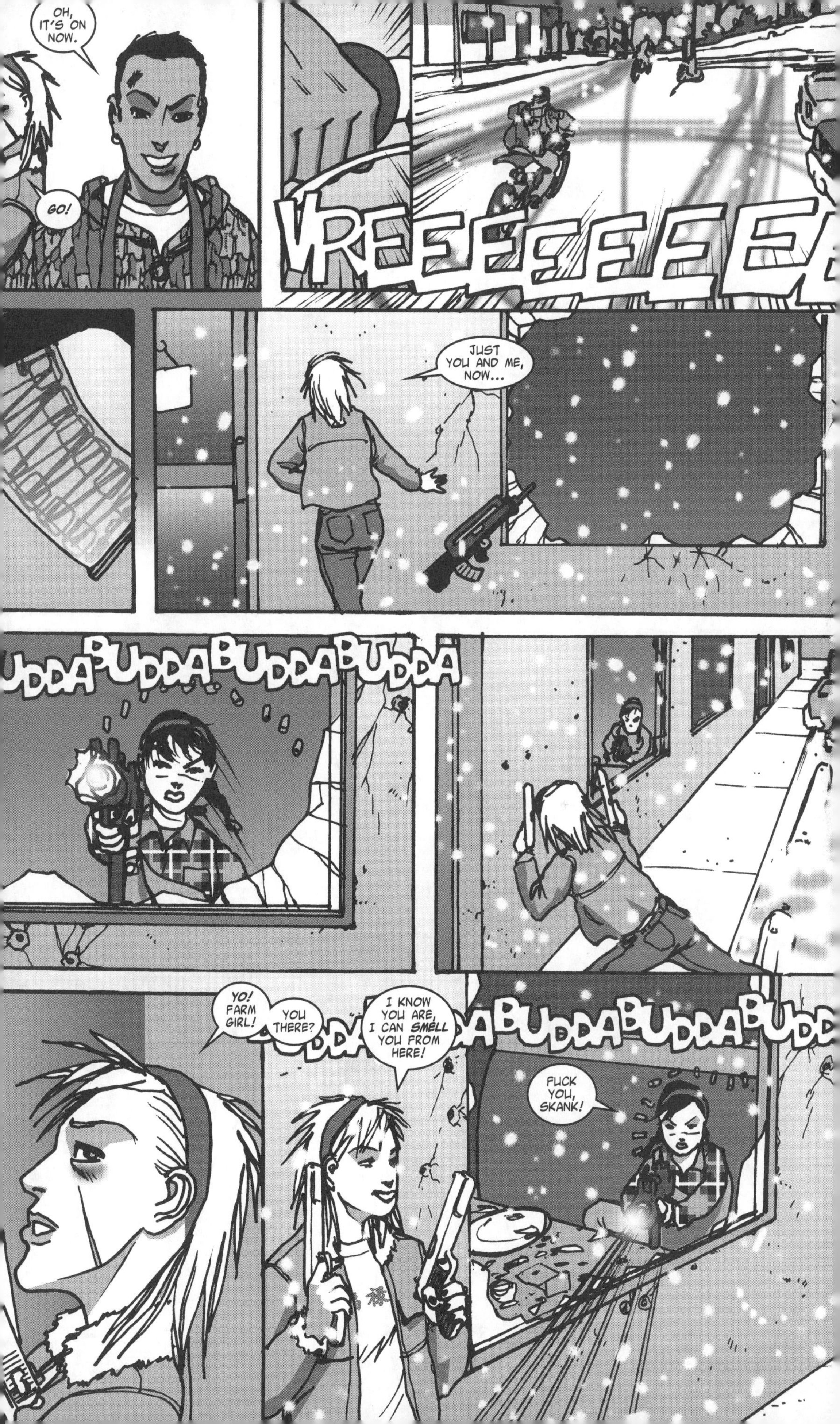
OH, IT'S ON NOW.
GO!
VREEEEEEEE
JUST YOU AND ME, NOW...
BUDDABUDDABUDDABUDDA
YO! FARM GIRL!
YOU THERE?
I KNOW YOU ARE, I CAN SMELL YOU FROM HERE!
BUDDABUDDABUDDABUDD
FUCK YOU, SKANK!

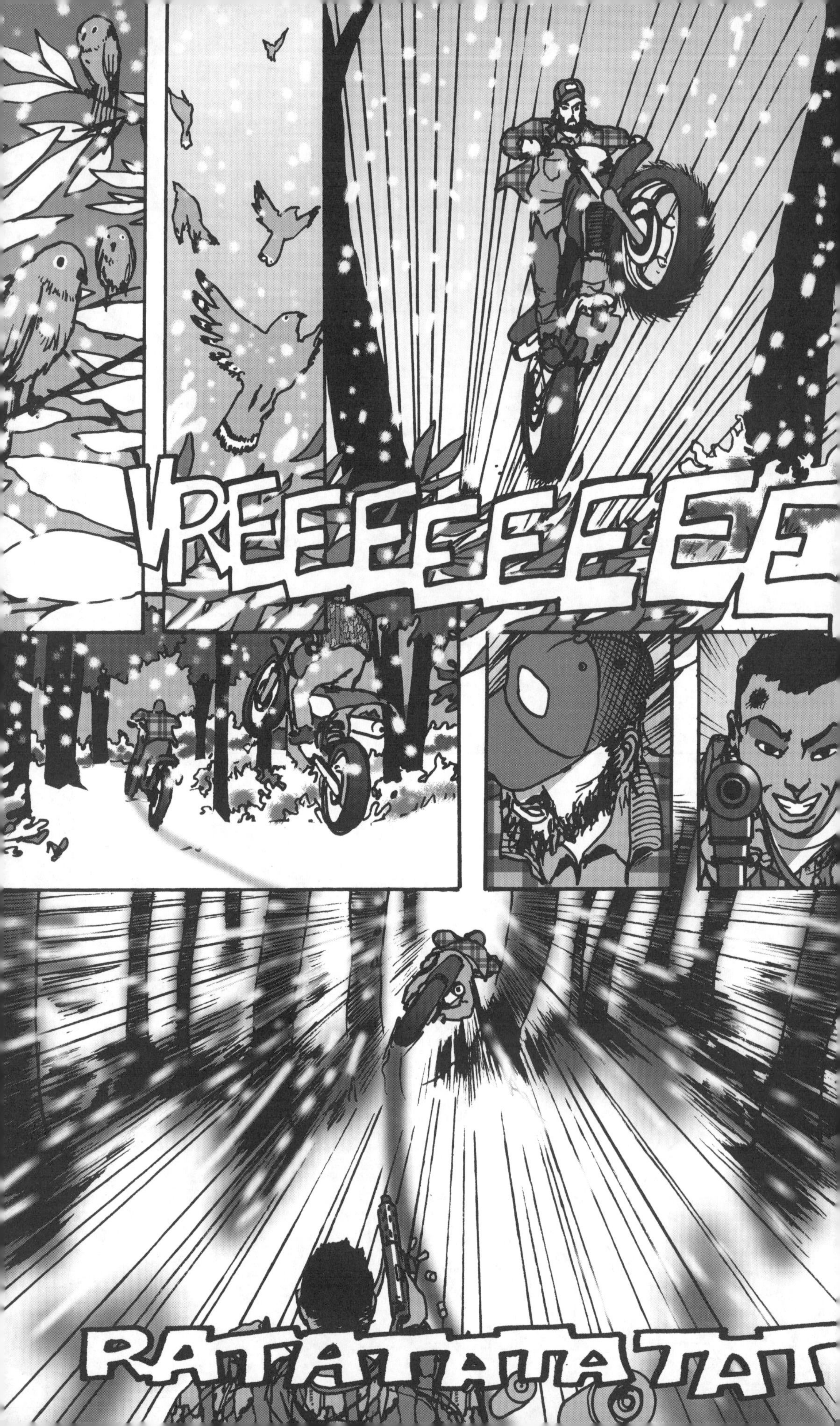
VREEEEEEEEE
RATATATATATAT

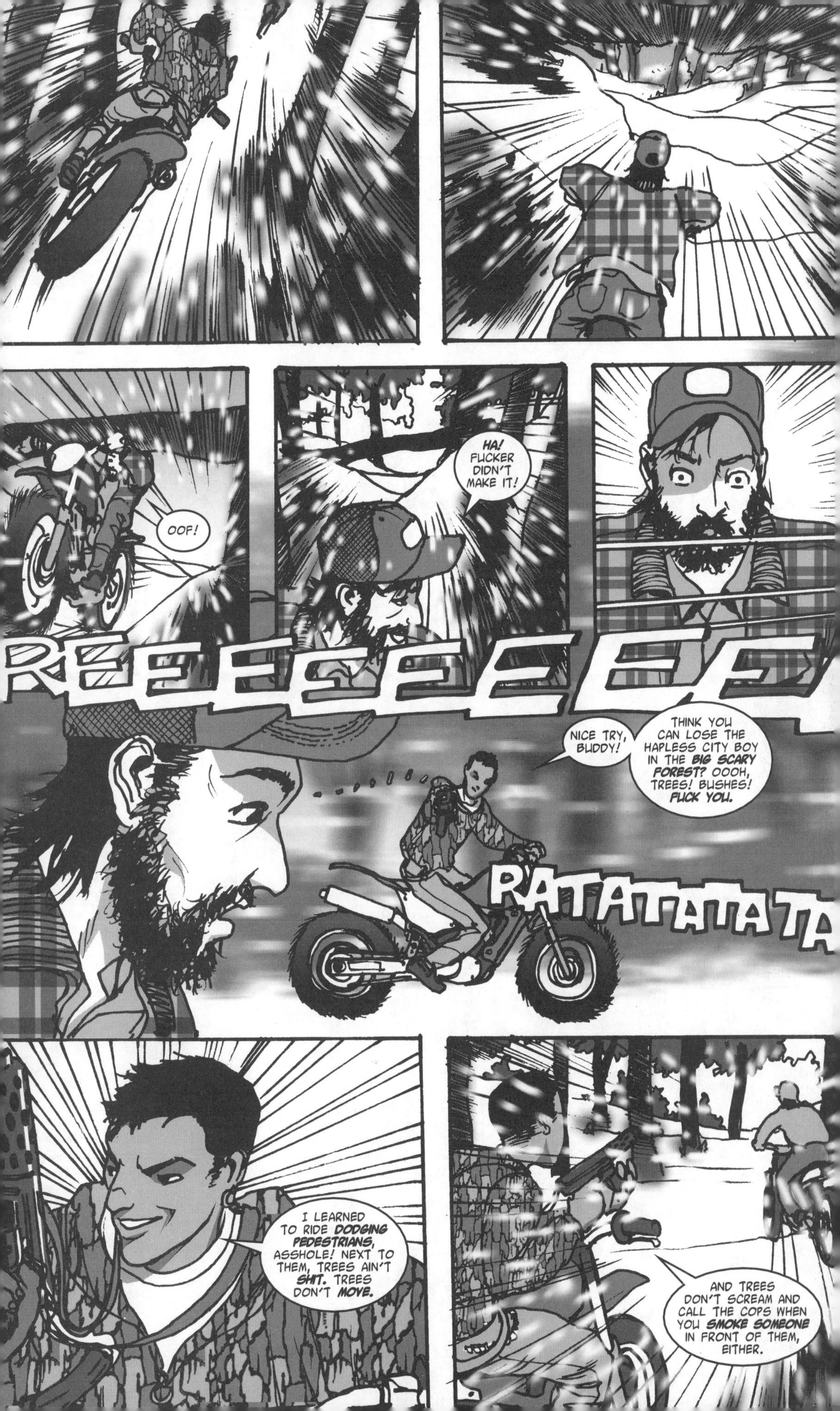
OOF!
HA! FUCKER DIDN'T MAKE IT!
REEEEEEEEE
NICE TRY, BUDDY!
THINK YOU CAN LOSE THE HAPLESS CITY BOY IN THE BIG SCARY FOREST? OOOH, TREES! BUSHES! FUCK YOU.
RATATATATA TA
I LEARNED TO RIDE DODGING PEDESTRIANS, ASSHOLE! NEXT TO THEM, TREES AIN'T SHIT. TREES DON'T MOVE.
AND TREES DON'T SCREAM AND CALL THE COPS WHEN YOU SMOKE SOMEONE IN FRONT OF THEM, EITHER.

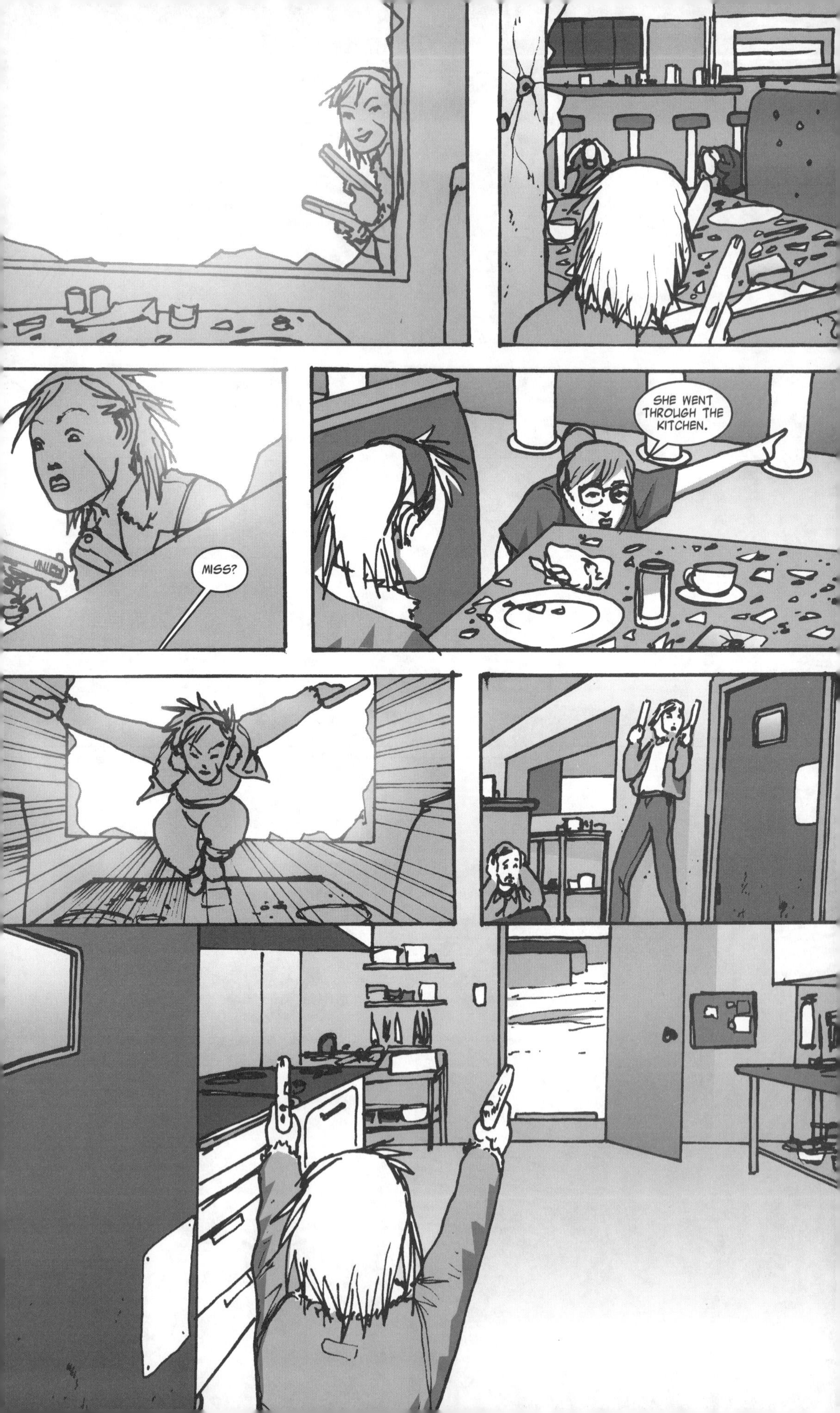
MISS?
SHE WENT THROUGH THE KITCHEN.

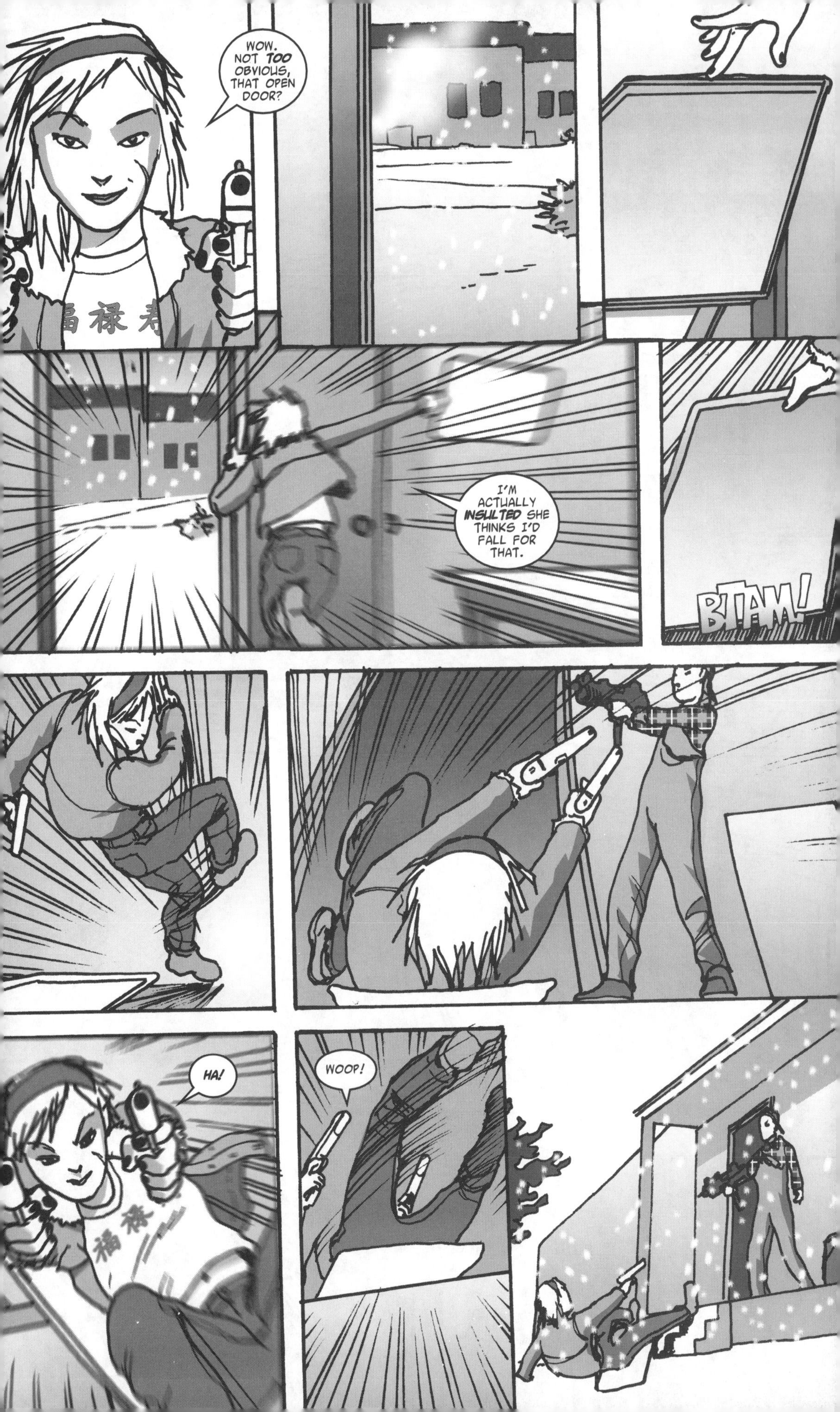
WOW. NOT TOO OBVIOUS, THAT OPEN DOOR?
I'M ACTUALLY INSULTED SHE THINKS I'D FALL FOR THAT.
BLAM!
HA!
WOOP!

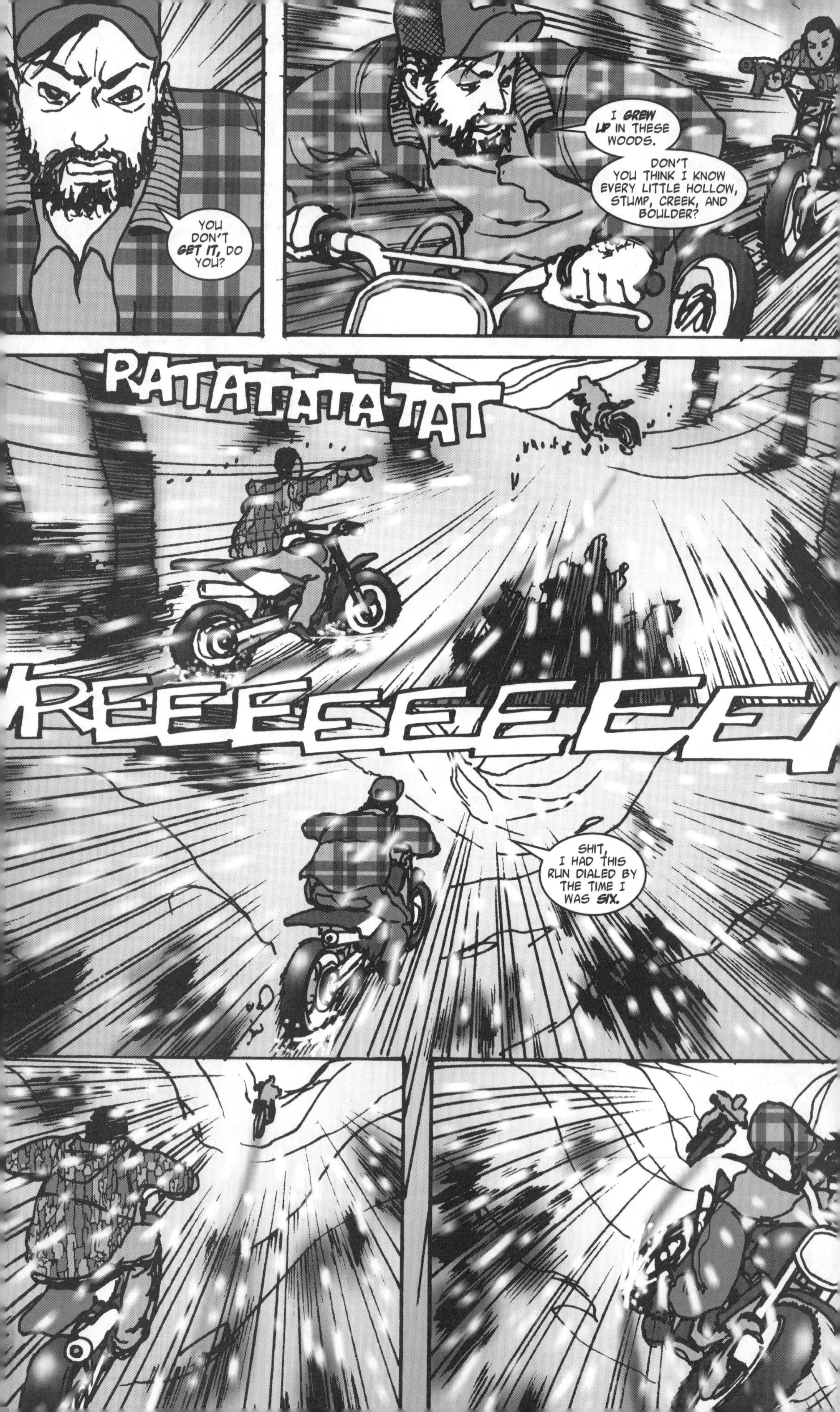
YOU DON'T GET IT, DO YOU?
I GREW UP IN THESE WOODS.
DON'T YOU THINK I KNOW EVERY LITTLE HOLLOW, STUMP, CREEK, AND BOULDER?
RATATATATAT
REEEEEEEEEE
SHIT, I HAD THIS RUN DIALED BY THE TIME I WAS SIX.

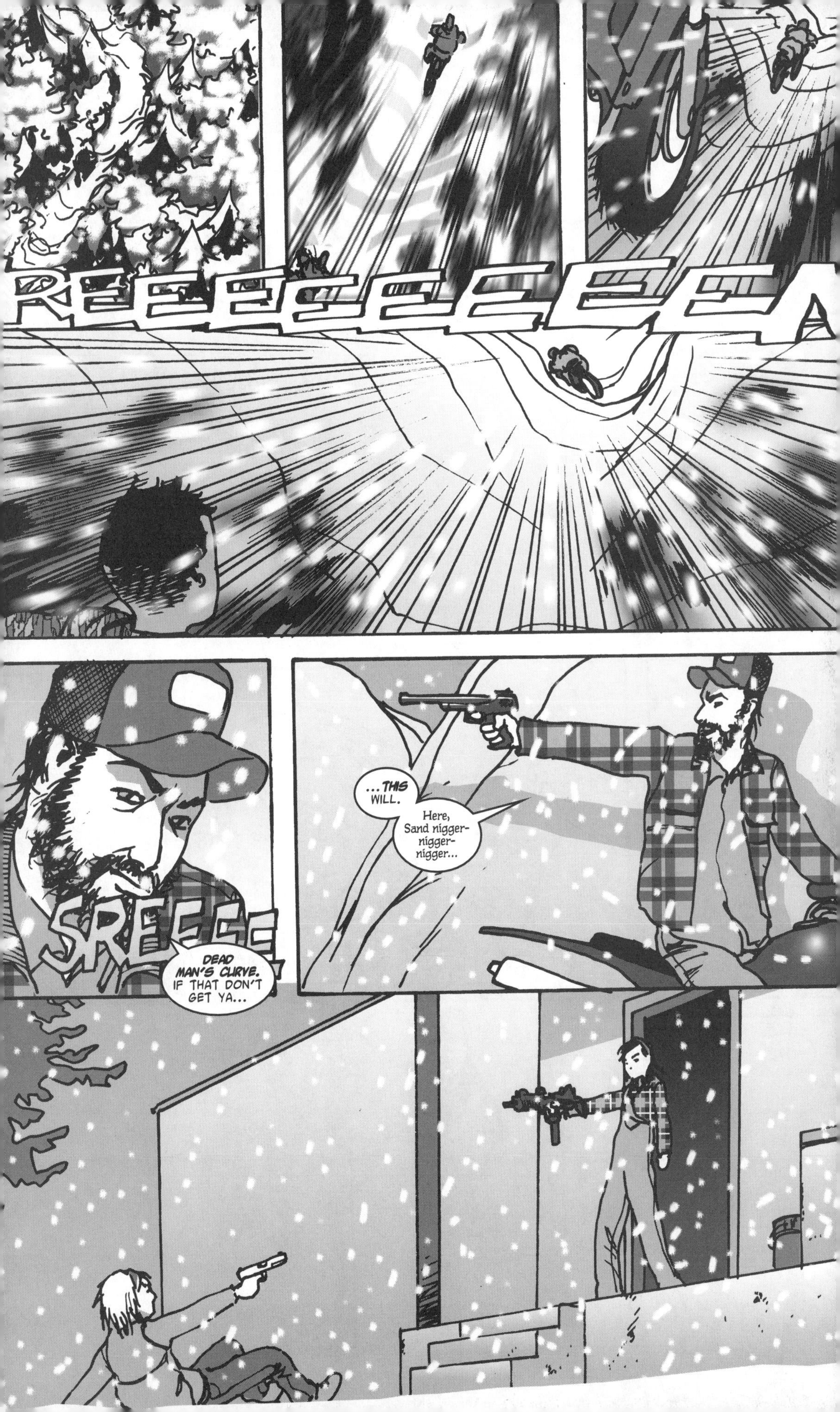
REEEEEEEEA
SREEEE
DEAD MAN'S CURVE. IF THAT DON'T GET YA...
...THIS WILL.
Here, Sand nigger-nigger-nigger...

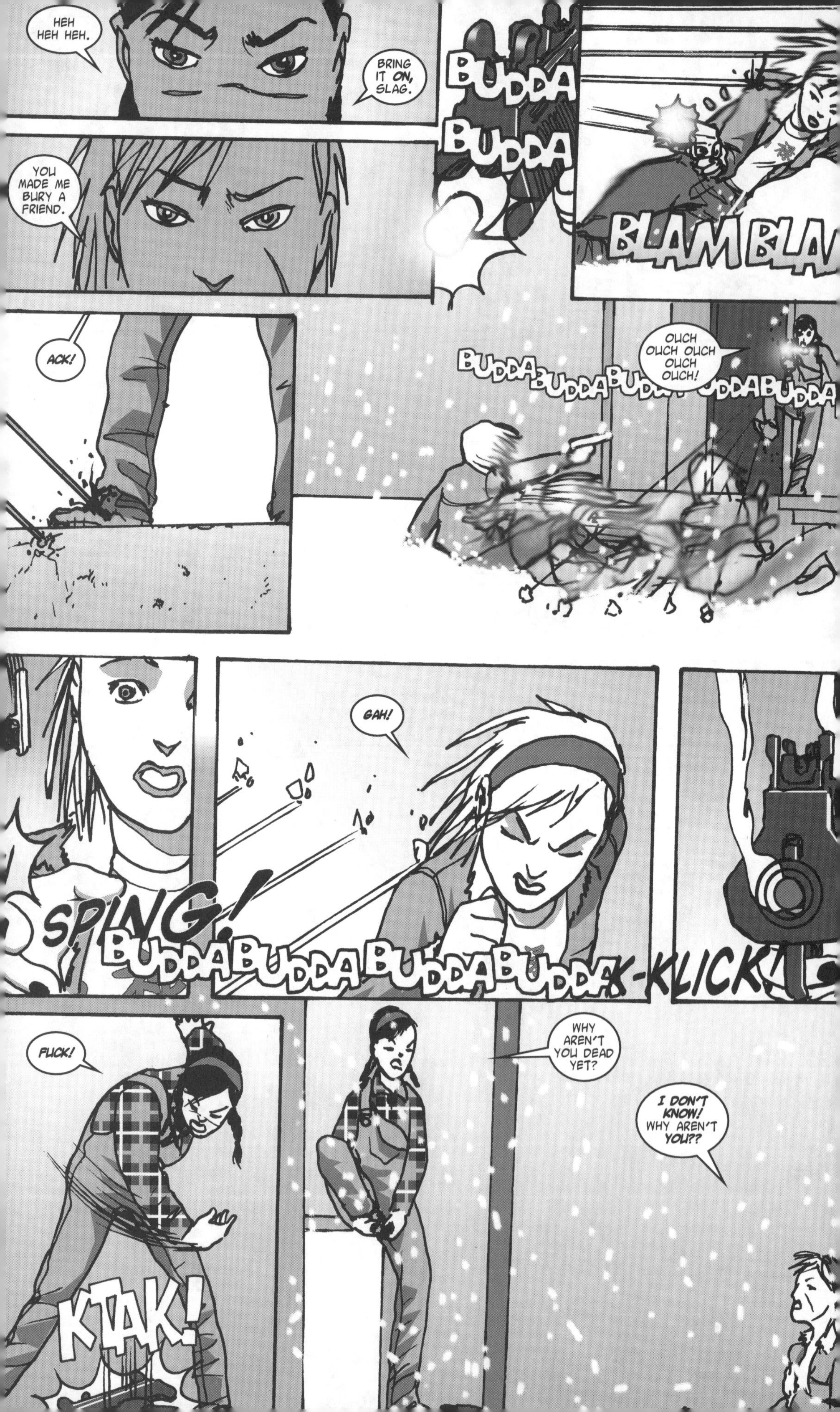
HEH HEH HEH.
BRING IT ON, SLAG.
YOU MADE ME BURY A FRIEND.
BUDDA BUDDA
BLAM BLA
ACK!
BUDDA BUDDA BUDD
OUCH OUCH OUCH OUCH OUCH!
UDDA BUDDA
GAH!
SPING!
BUDDA BUDDA BUDDA BUDDA
K-KLICK!
FUCK!
KTAK!
WHY AREN'T YOU DEAD YET?
I DON'T KNOW! WHY AREN'T YOU??

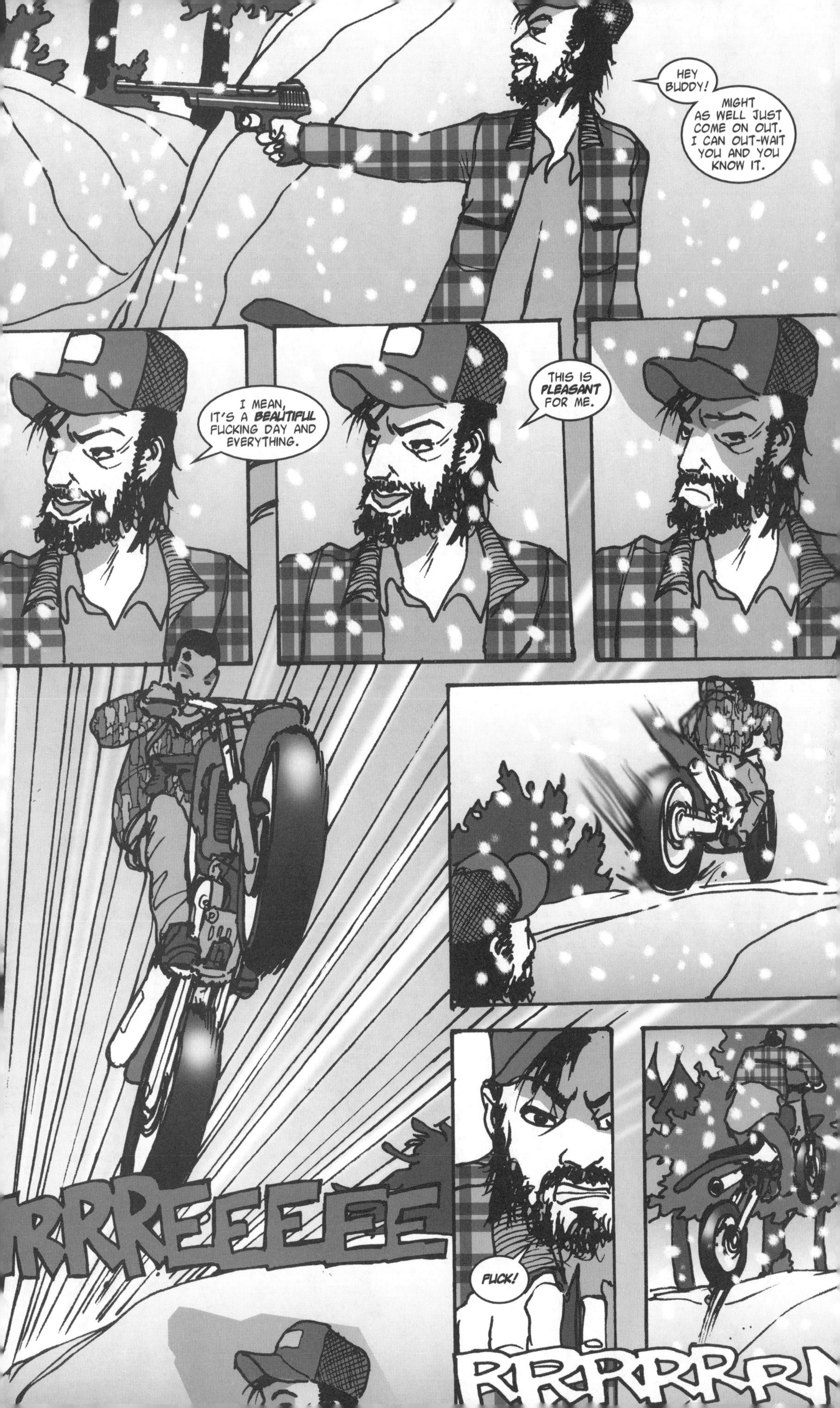
HEY BUDDY!
MIGHT AS WELL JUST COME ON OUT. I CAN OUT-WAIT YOU AND YOU KNOW IT.
I MEAN, IT'S A **BEAUTIFUL** FUCKING DAY AND EVERYTHING.
THIS IS **PLEASANT** FOR ME.
RRREEEEEE
FUCK!
RRRRRRN

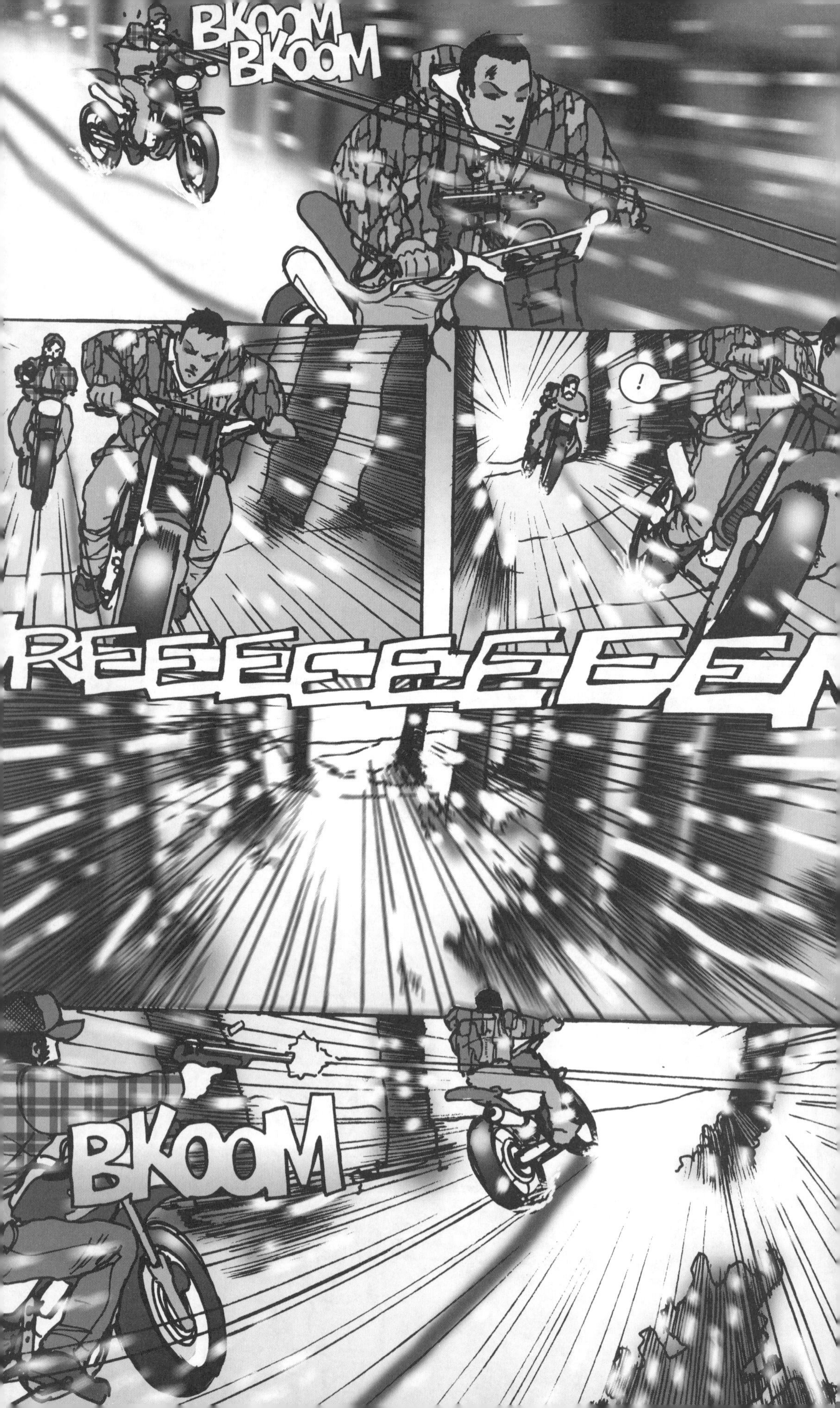
BKOOM BKOOM
!
REEEEEEEEEN
BKOOM

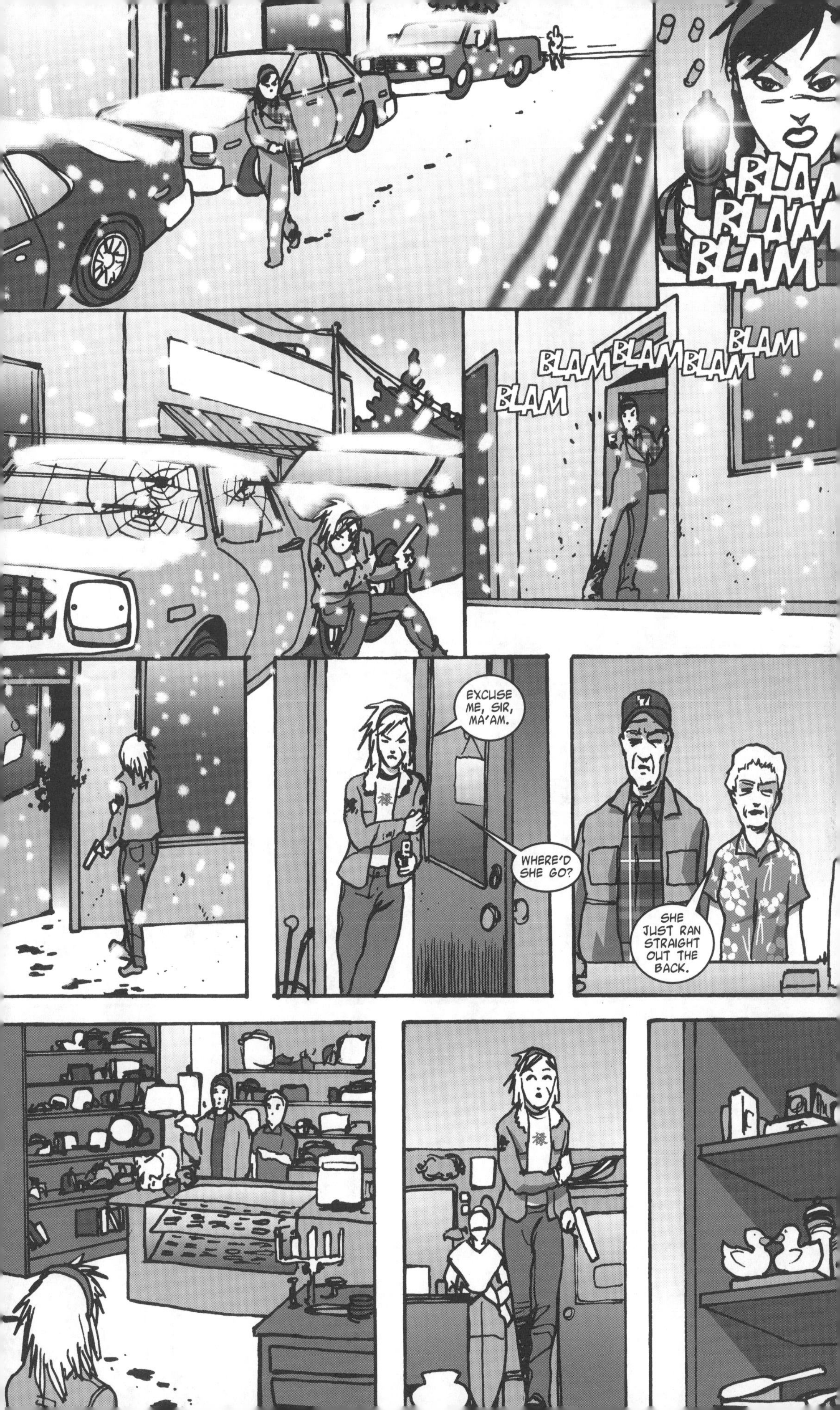
BLAM
BLAM
BLAM
BLAM
BLAM
BLAM
BLAM
BLAM
EXCUSE ME, SIR, MA'AM.
WHERE'D SHE GO?
SHE JUST RAN STRAIGHT OUT THE BACK.

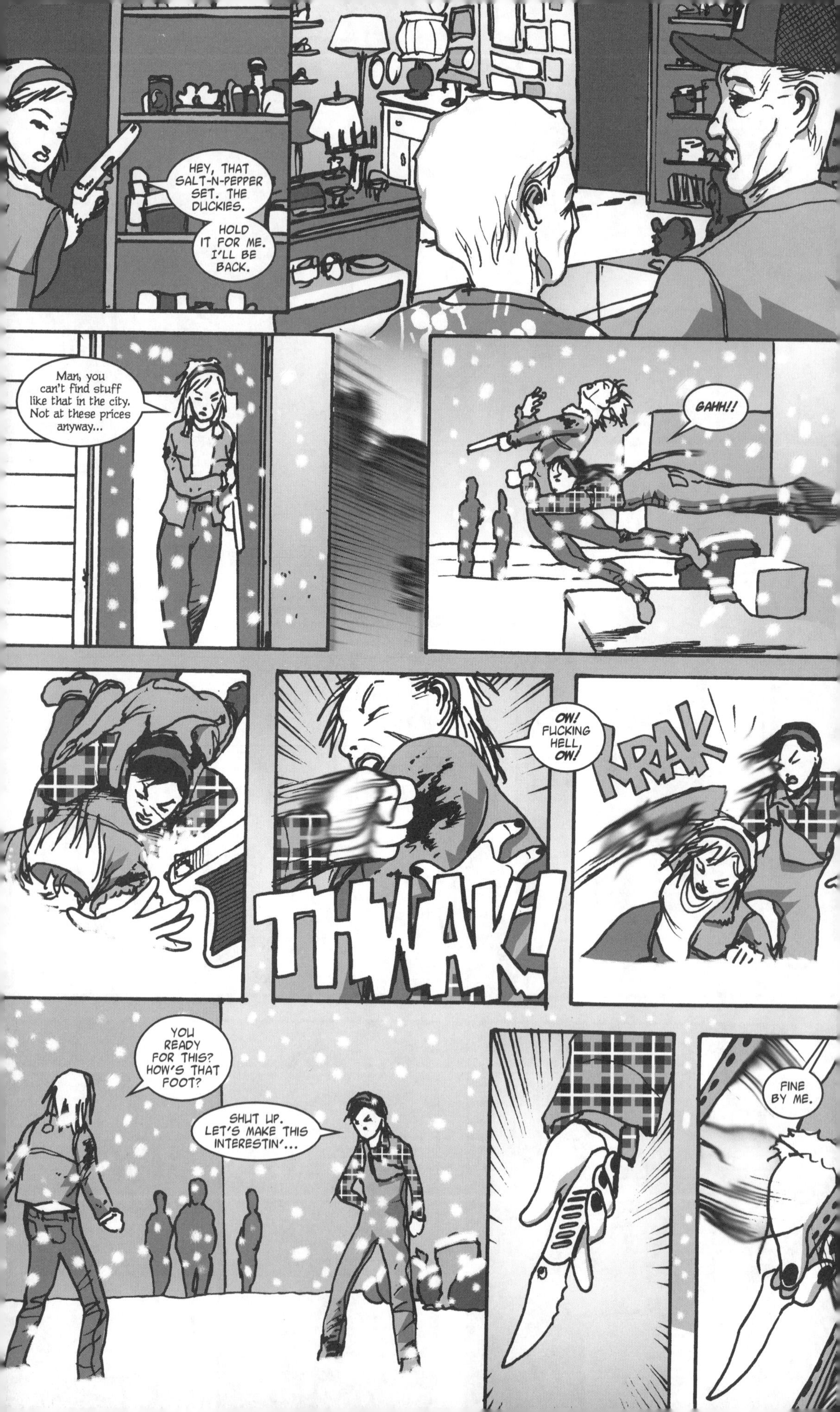
HEY, THAT SALT-N-PEPPER SET. THE DUCKIES.
HOLD IT FOR ME. I'LL BE BACK.
Man, you can't find stuff like that in the city. Not at these prices anyway...
GAHH!!
THWAK!
OW! FUCKING HELL, OW!
KRAK
YOU READY FOR THIS? HOW'S THAT FOOT?
SHUT UP. LET'S MAKE THIS INTERESTIN'...
FINE BY ME.

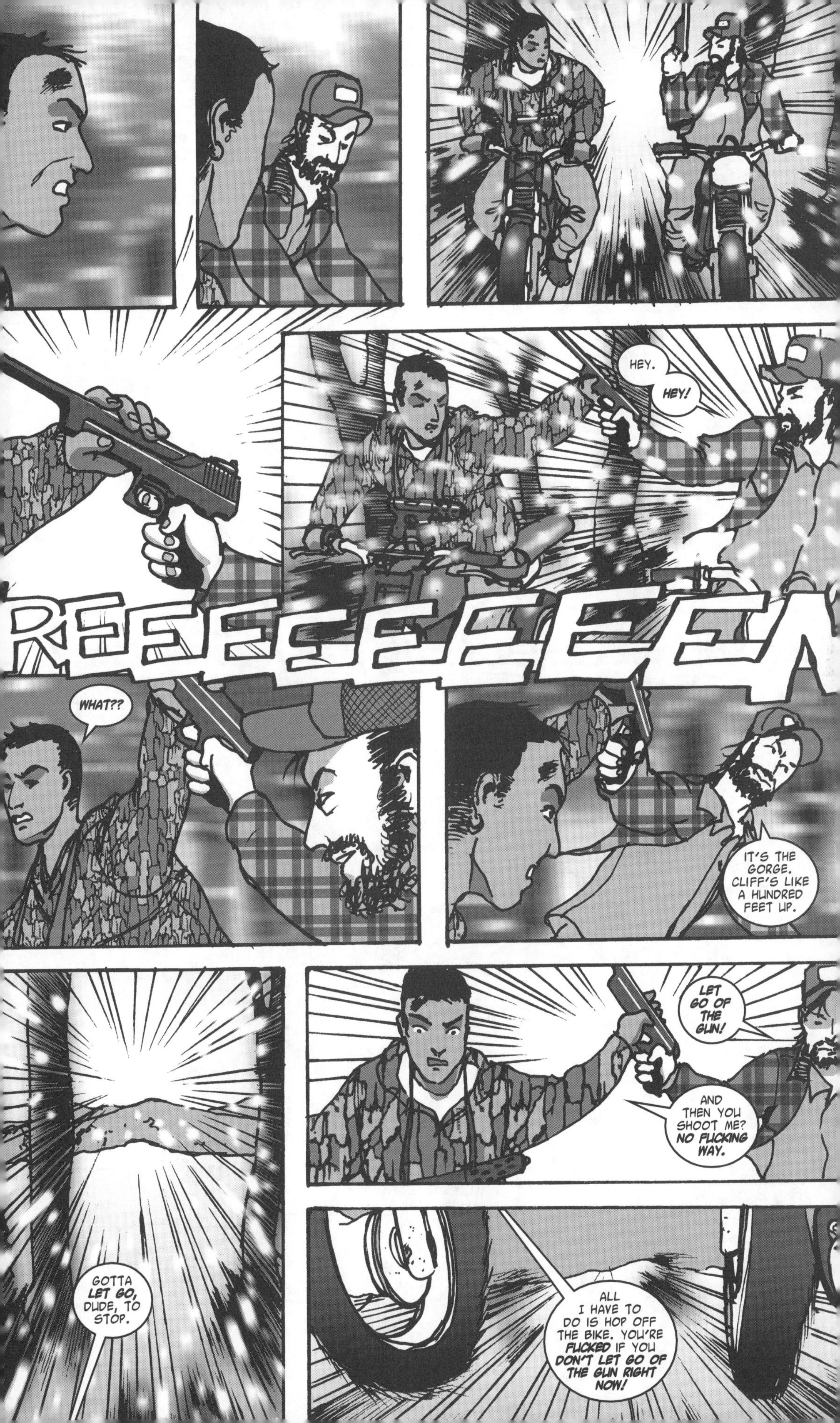
HEY.
HEY!
REEEEEEEEEN
WHAT??
IT'S THE GORGE. CLIFF'S LIKE A HUNDRED FEET UP.
GOTTA LET GO, DUDE, TO STOP.
LET GO OF THE GUN!
AND THEN YOU SHOOT ME? NO FUCKING WAY.
ALL I HAVE TO DO IS HOP OFF THE BIKE. YOU'RE FUCKED IF YOU DON'T LET GO OF THE GUN RIGHT NOW!

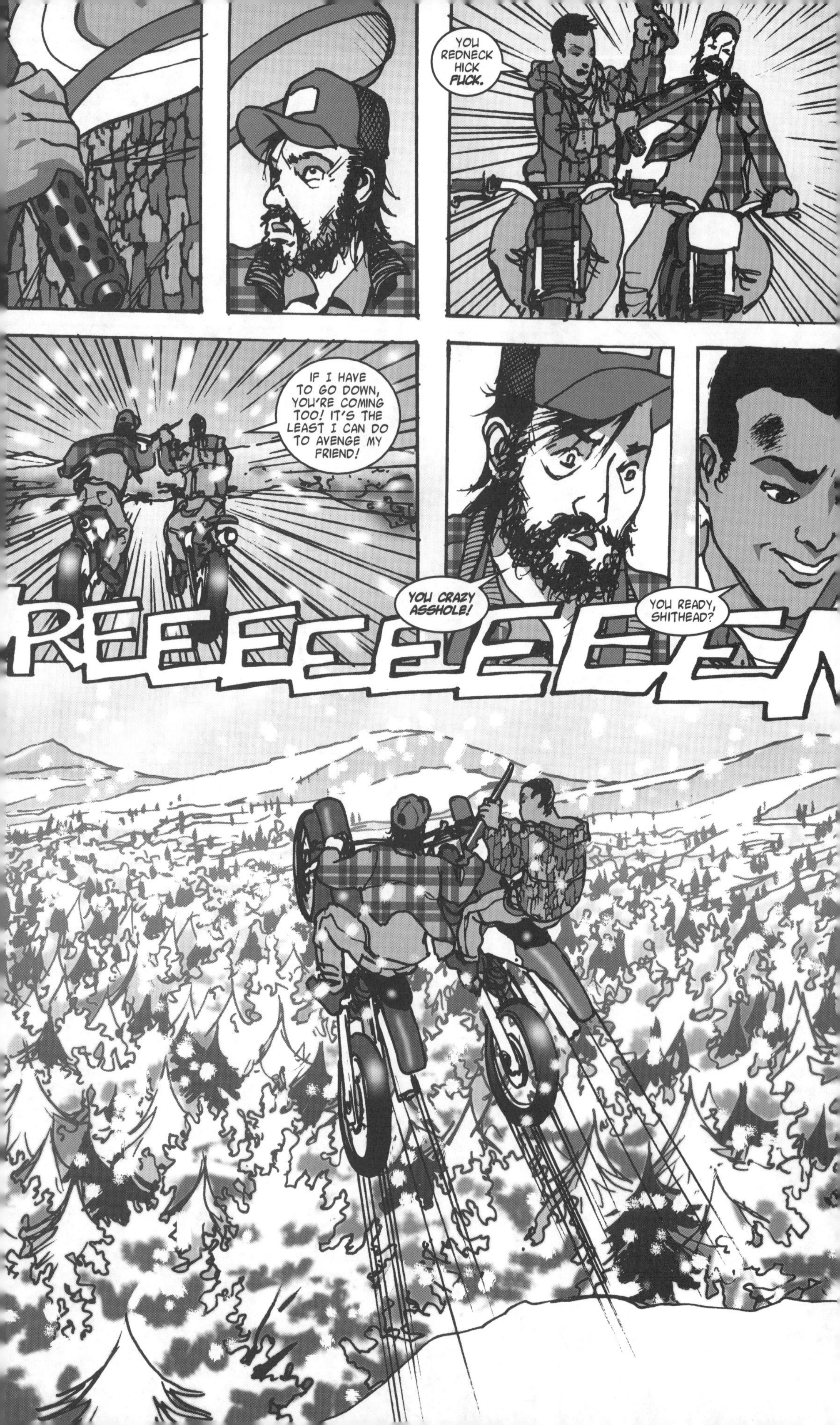
YOU REDNECK HICK FUCK.
IF I HAVE TO GO DOWN, YOU'RE COMING TOO! IT'S THE LEAST I CAN DO TO AVENGE MY FRIEND!
YOU CRAZY ASSHOLE!
YOU READY, SHITHEAD?
REEEEEEEEN

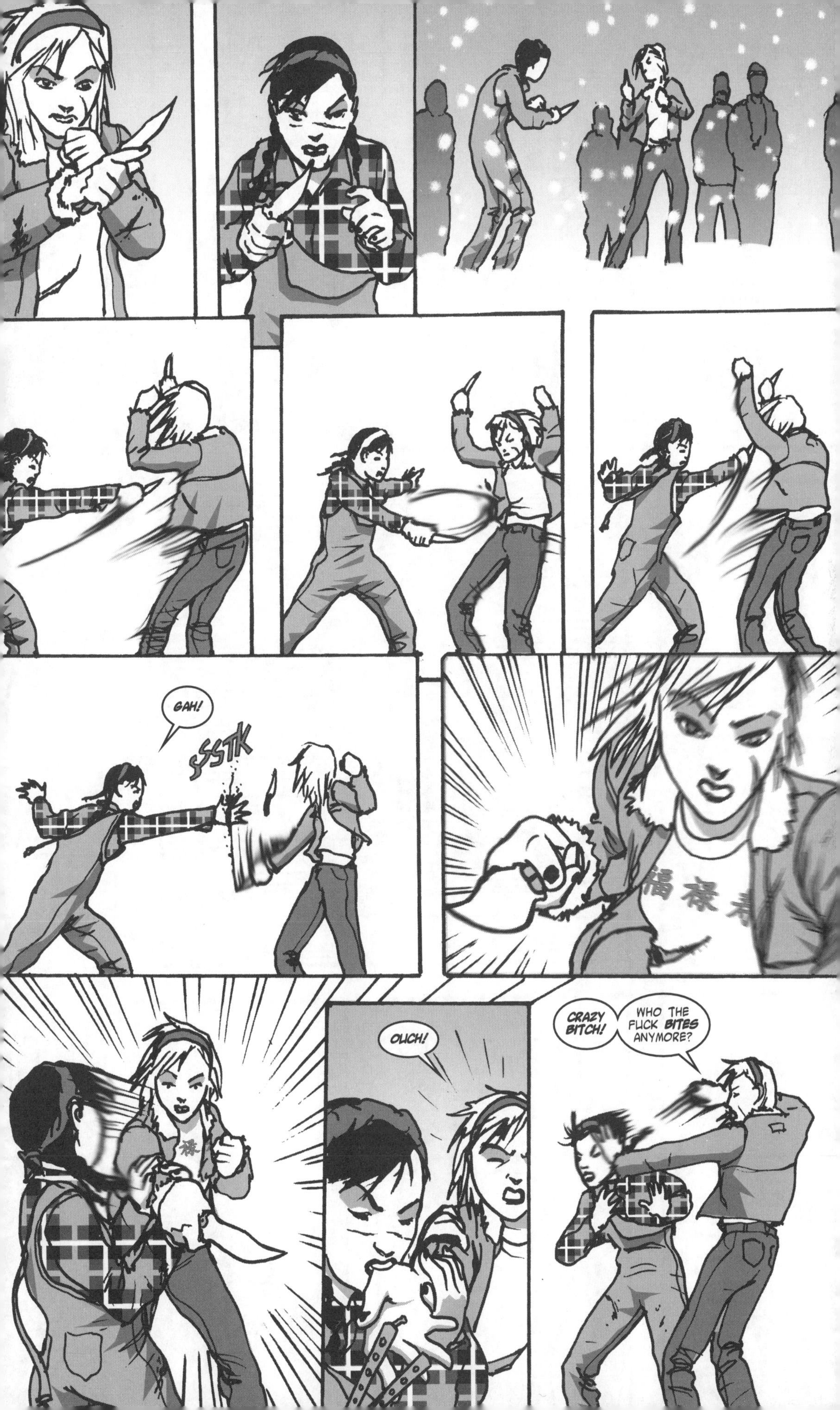
GAH!
SSSTK
OUCH!
CRAZY BITCH!
WHO THE FUCK BITES ANYMORE?

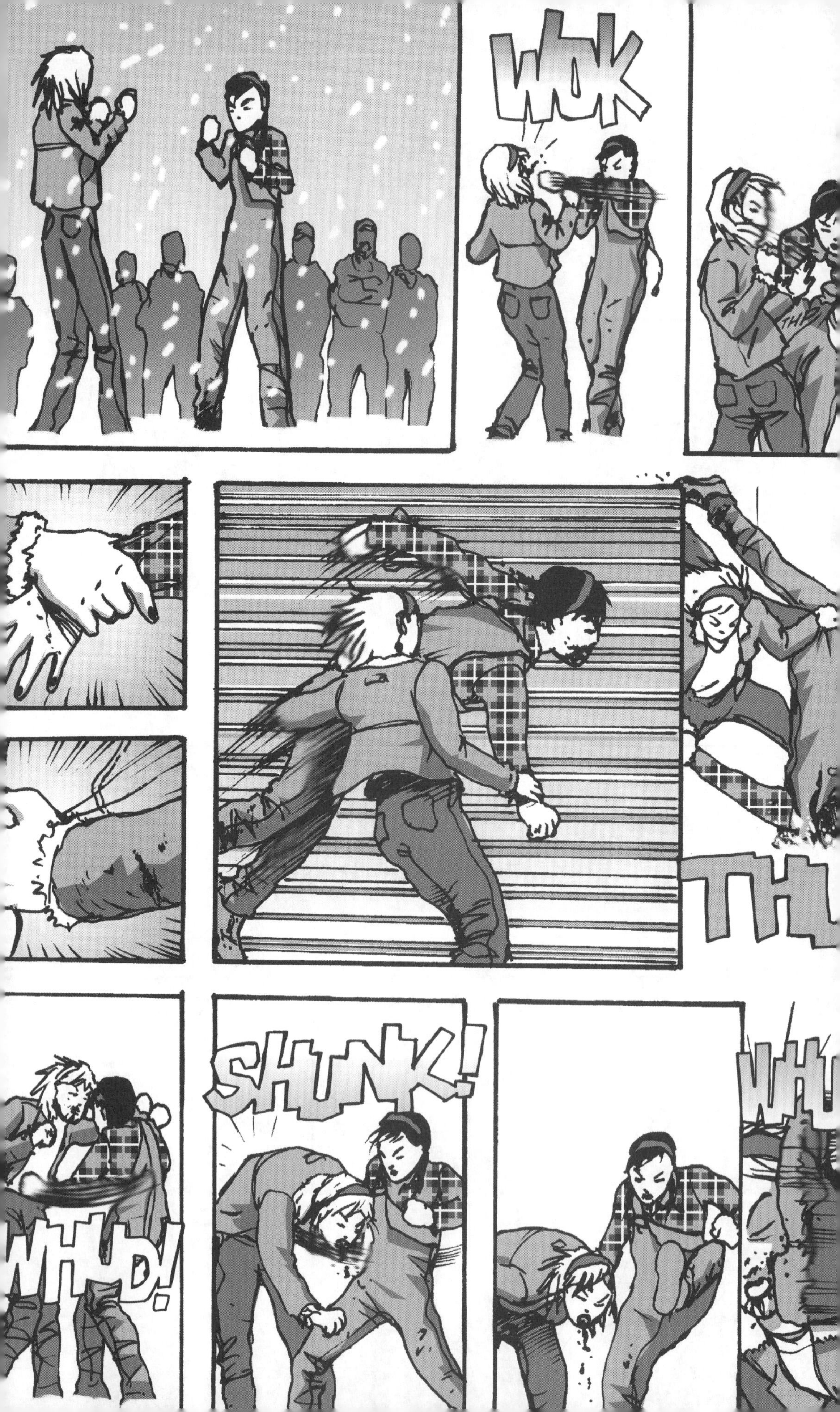
WOK
THP
THU
WHUD!
SHUNK!
WHU

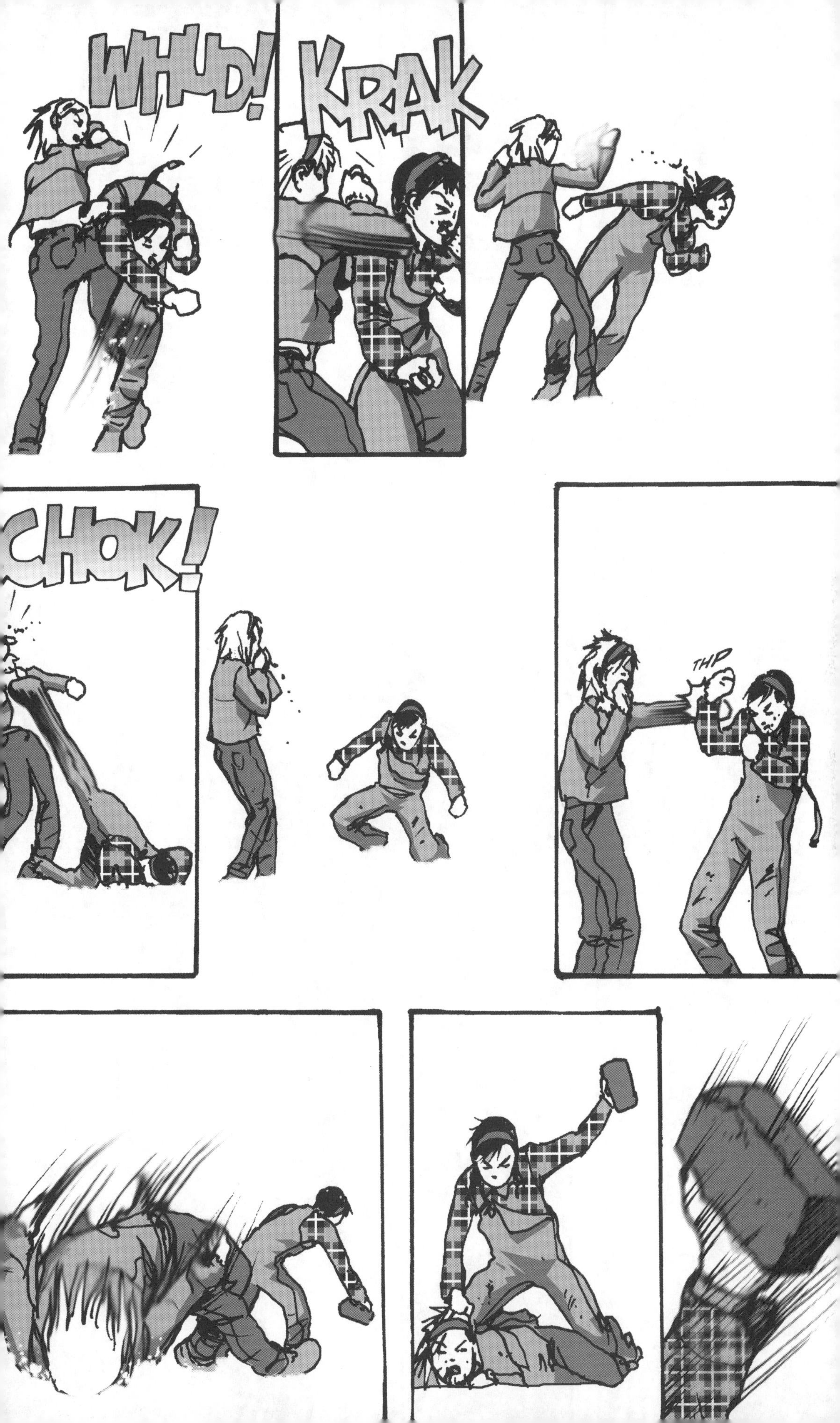
WHUD!
KRAK
CHOK!
THP

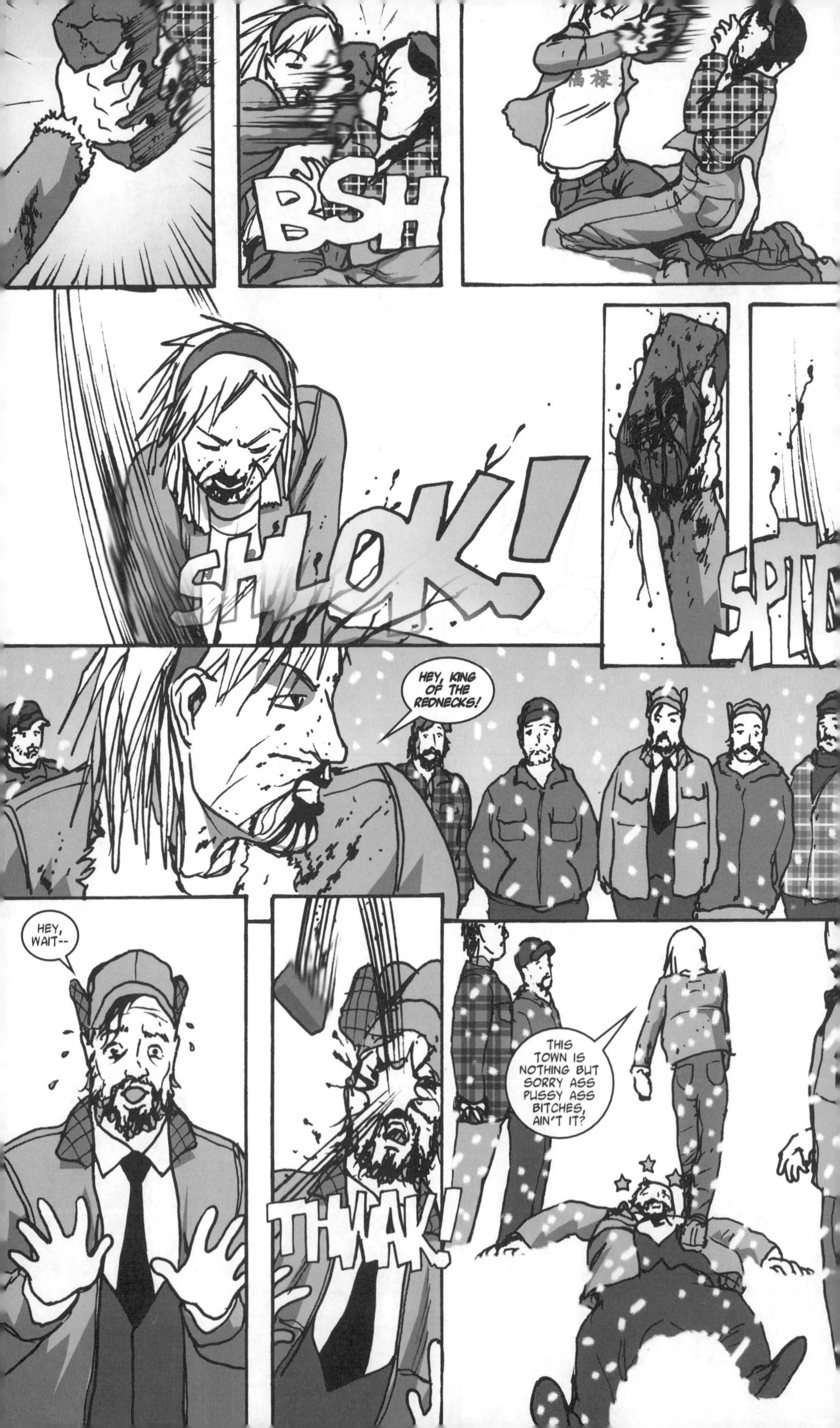
BSH
SHLOK!
SPLO
HEY, KING OF THE REDNECKS!
HEY, WAIT--
THWAK!
THIS TOWN IS NOTHING BUT SORRY ASS PUSSY ASS BITCHES, AIN'T IT?

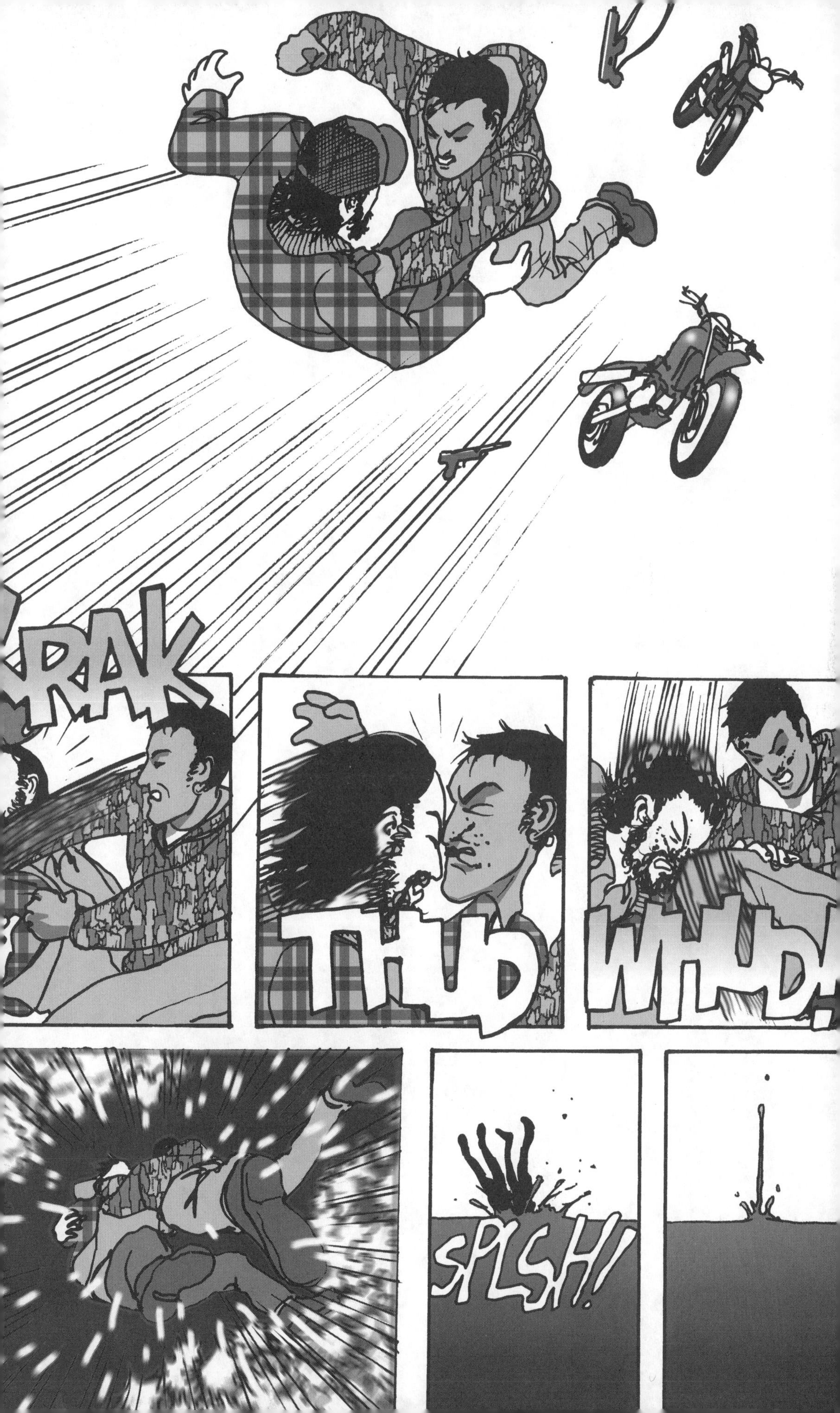
RAK
THUD
SPLSH!

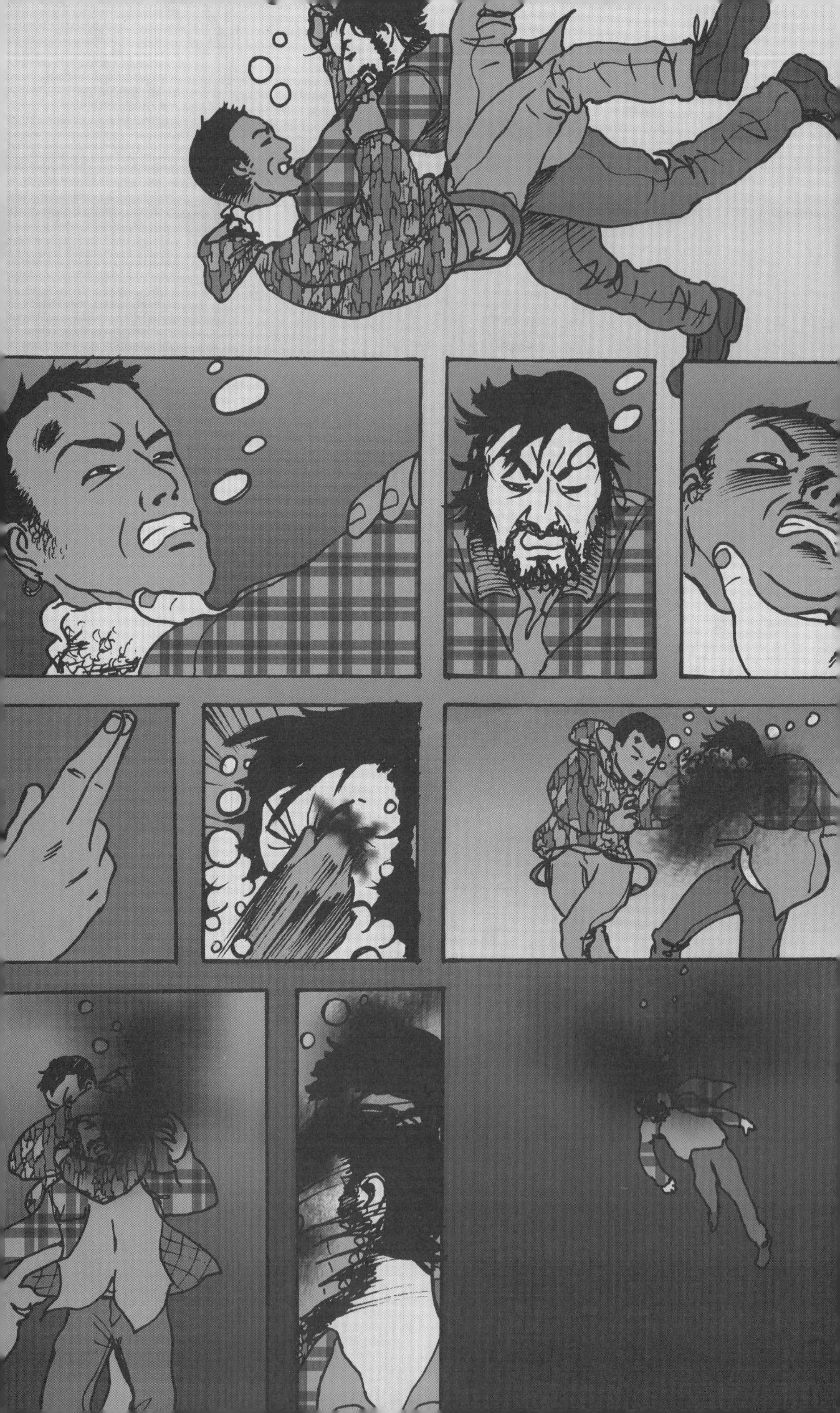

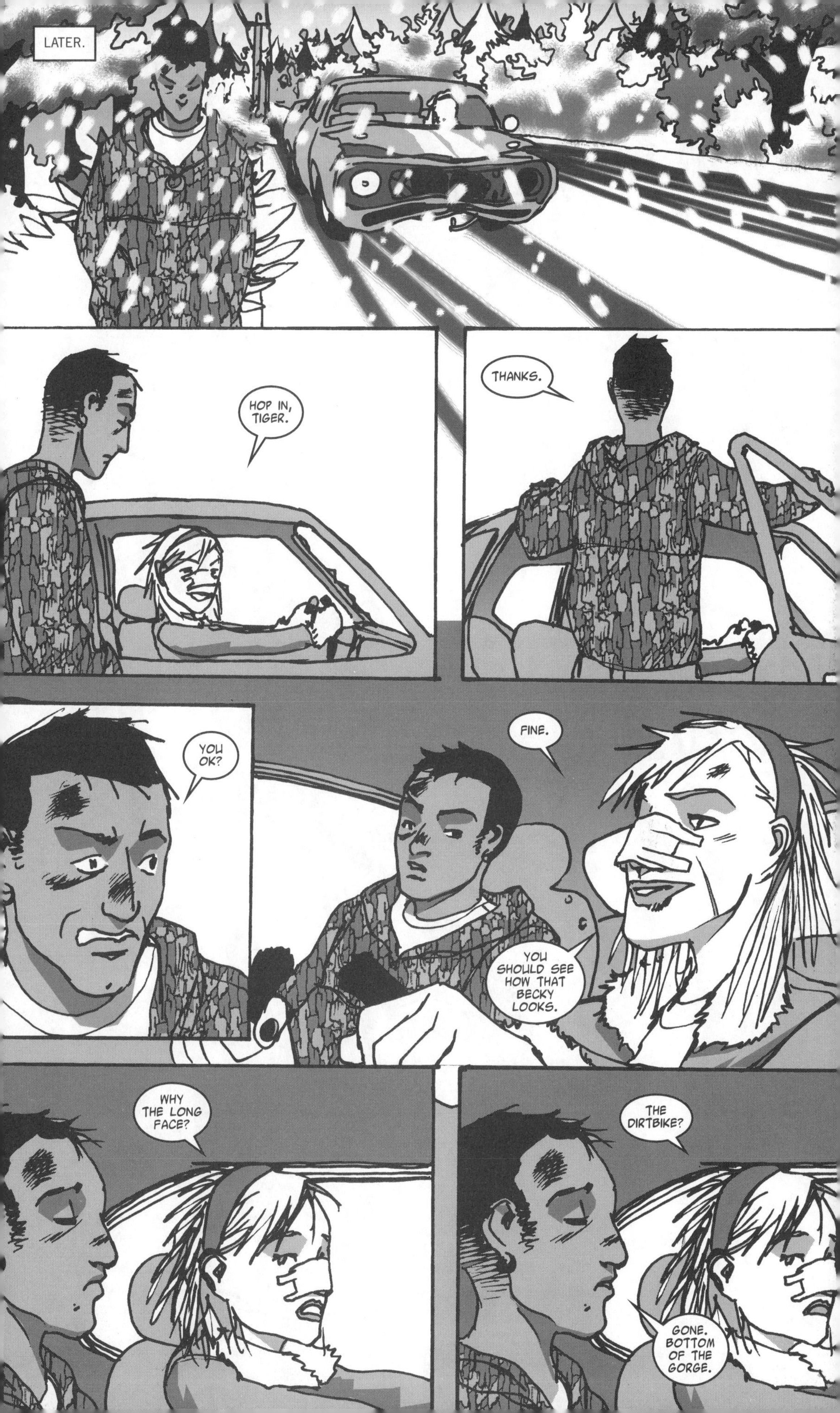
LATER.
HOP IN, TIGER.
THANKS.
YOU OK?
FINE.
YOU SHOULD SEE HOW THAT BECKY LOOKS.
WHY THE LONG FACE?
THE DIRTBIKE?
GONE. BOTTOM OF THE GORGE.

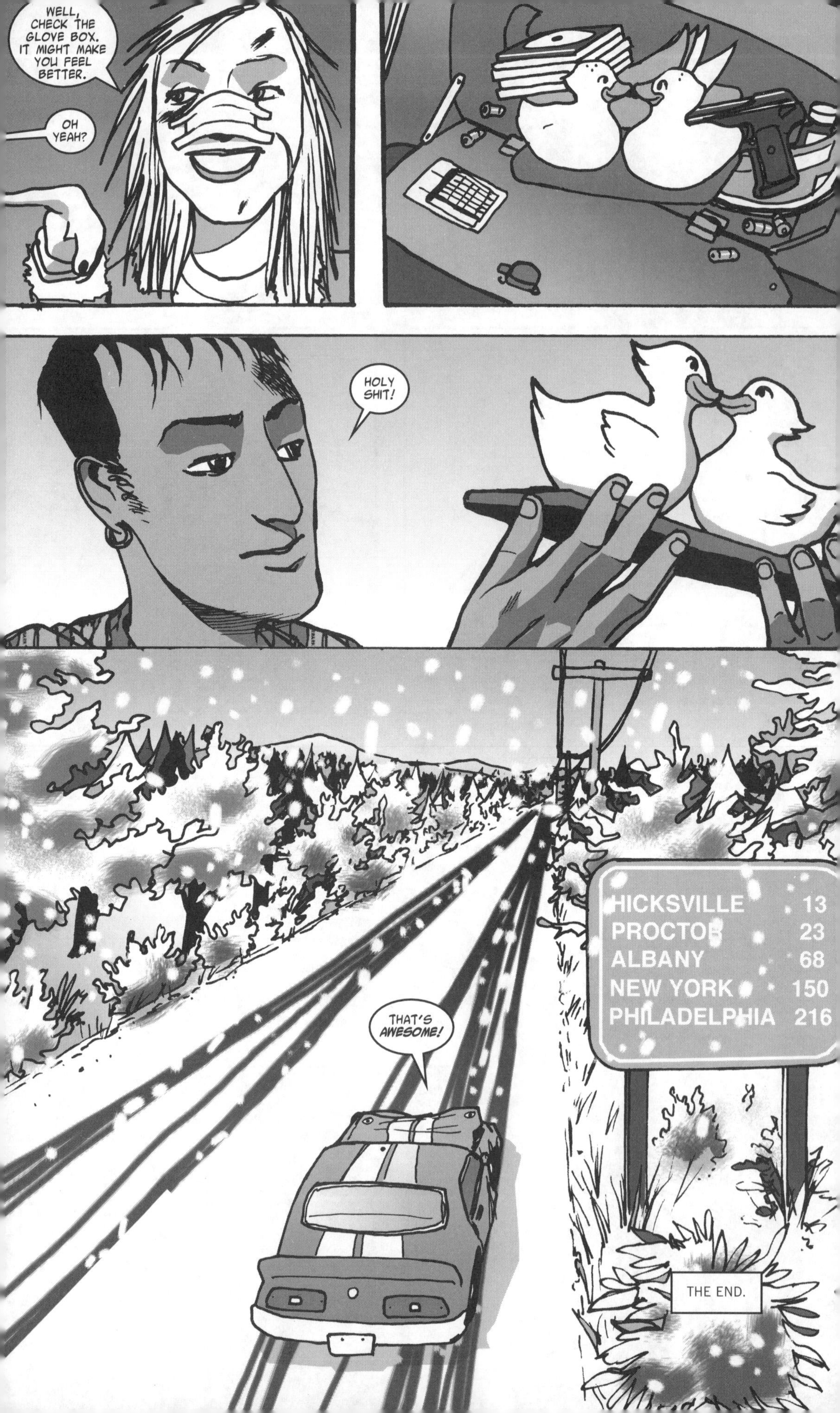

WELL, CHECK THE GLOVE BOX. IT MIGHT MAKE YOU FEEL BETTER.
OH YEAH?
HOLY SHIT!
HICKSVILLE 13
PROCTOR 23
ALBANY 68
NEW YORK 150
PHILADELPHIA 216
THAT'S AWESOME!
THE END.

# THE LOWDOWN NO GOOD REDNECK MOTHERFUCKERS RESPONSIBLE:

**BRIAN WOOD** Born and raised and in Northern Vermont, Brian hates (yet secretly loves) his old hick neighbors so much so he had to write this book and dis (pay loving tribute to) them all. Brian lives in San Francisco now, writes and draws shitloads of comics, designs t-shirts, and drinks beer for breakfast. *www.brianwood.com*

**ROB G** is a sequential artist who has worked for DC comics, Humanoids publishing, as well as the self-published comic Teenagers from Mars with writer Rick Spears. He also wrote and drew a short story for the SPX 2003 Anthology. He lives in Brooklyn and is fireproof. *www.robg.com*

**RYAN YOUNT** longs for the day when he can spend all his time working on machines. But drawing, writing, lettering, and coordinating the production of comics for AiT/Planet Lar is a pretty damn good gig. Plus, there's that critically-acclaimed Scurvy Dogs comic he does with Andrew Boyd. So, he's got that going for him. Which is good. *www.scurvy-dogs.com*